heavenly chocolate desserts

heavenly chocolate desserts

tarts, mousses, brownies and more

RYLAND
PETERS
& SMALL

LONDON NEW YORK

**Essex County
Council Libraries**

First published in Great Britain in 2008
by Ryland Peters & Small
20–21 Jockey's Fields
London WC1R 4BW
www.rylandpeters.com

10 9 8 7 6 5 4 3 2 1

ISBN 978 1 84597 727 6

A catalogue record for this book is
available from the British Library.

Printed and bound in China

Editor Céline Hughes

Picture Research Emily Westlake

Production Manager Patricia Harrington

Art Director Leslie Harrington

Publishing Director Alison Starling

Indexer Sandra Shotter

Notes

• All spoon measurements are level
unless otherwise stated.

• Ovens should be preheated to the
specified temperature. Recipes in this
book were tested using a conventional
oven. If using a fan oven, cooking times
should be changed according to the
manufacturer's instructions.

• All eggs are medium, unless otherwise
specified. It is generally recommended
that free-range eggs be used. Recipes
containing raw or partially cooked egg,
or raw fish or shellfish, should not be
served to the very young, very old, anyone
with a compromised immune system or
pregnant women.

contents

introduction

We've all done it – reached for that chocolate bar when the going gets tough. In fact, for centuries we've known and cherished the mood-enhancing effects of cocoa. So it's no surprise that there's something about a chocolate dessert at the end of a meal that puts a smile on your face and, inexplicably, makes you feel better equipped to deal with life. Whether it's a good old-fashioned brownie with a generous scoop of luxurious vanilla ice cream, a simple chocolate mousse, a suave Sachertorte or an utterly outrageous pain au chocolat pudding, chocolate is so versatile an ingredient that there are countless ways of serving it up, no matter what mood you're in or what occasion you're catering for.

Just as you should always have flour, eggs and sugar in your kitchen, ready to whip up a batch of biscuits for an impromptu afternoon visitor, make sure you have some fine cooking chocolate in the cupboard too. There's nothing like chocolate crèmes brûlées or marbled chocolate cheesecake to butter up a friend or wow your dinner guests.

So whether you're after something sticky, gooey, chilled, creamy, crispy, elegant, naughty, comforting, rich or smooth, there's a heavenly dessert here to have you licking every last trace of delicious chocolate from your plate (and wishing you'd never invited those people to share it with you).

hot puddings

This luscious crumble is sophisticated enough for the best dinner party. Chocolate and pears were made for each other – here the chocolate melts and mixes with the pear juice to make a delicious sauce. Pumpernickel makes an interestingly crunchy topping, and gives the dessert a dramatic look.

pear and chocolate crumble

2–3 large, not-too-ripe pears

50 g caster sugar

2–3 tablespoons powdered dark drinking chocolate (not cocoa powder) or grated dark chocolate

finely grated zest of ½ unwaxed lemon

pouring cream or chocolate ice cream, to serve

choco-pumpernickel topping

100 g sliced pumpernickel

100 g stale brown bread

4 tablespoons powdered dark drinking chocolate (not cocoa powder) or grated dark chocolate

50 g unsalted butter, chilled

75 g demerara sugar

a medium, shallow, ovenproof dish

SERVES 4

Preheat the oven to 180°C (350°F) Gas 4 and set a baking tray on the middle shelf to heat.

Peel, core and slice (or chop) the pears and put them in the ovenproof dish so that they fill it by two-thirds. Sprinkle the sugar, drinking chocolate (or grated chocolate, if using) and lemon zest over the top and mix well to coat the pears. Cover and set aside.

To make the topping, tear up the pumpernickel and brown bread and put in the bowl of a food processor. Pulse for a minute or so until very roughly crumbed. Add the drinking chocolate (or grated chocolate if using), butter and sugar and pulse again for a minute or so until finer crumbs form. Do not overprocess or it will form a solid lump. Pop in a plastic bag and chill until needed.

When ready to cook the crumble, uncover the pears and sprinkle lightly and evenly with the topping mixture. Place the ovenproof dish on the baking tray in the preheated oven and bake for 25–30 minutes, or until the pears are very tender and the top nice and crisp.

Remove from the oven and serve warm with pouring cream or a scoop of chocolate ice cream.

This is a delicious, creamy risotto based on an ancient recipe from the north-east coast of Sicily.
It is variously flavoured with vanilla, cinnamon and chilli (a flavour beloved by Sicilians).
A pinch of ground chilli in the pudding adds a warmth and mysterious flavour – for adults only.

dark chocolate risotto

3 tablespoons unsweetened
cocoa powder

100 g sugar

¼ teaspoon ground cinnamon

900 ml whole milk

150 g risotto rice,
preferably *vialone nano*

3 long strips of unwaxed
orange zest

100 g bitter dark chocolate, grated

75 g chopped candied orange peel
(optional)

to serve

cinnamon sticks

candied orange peel

icing sugar

pouring cream

4 small bowls or cups, warmed

SERVES 4

Put the cocoa, sugar and cinnamon in a small bowl and add 4 tablespoons of the milk. Mix until well blended, then add another 4 tablespoons of the milk.

Put the rice in a medium saucepan and stir in the cocoa-flavoured milk, the remaining milk and the strips of orange zest. Slowly bring to the boil, then reduce the heat, cover and barely simmer for 20 minutes. The rice should be very tender, creamy and slightly sloppy (if not, add a little extra hot milk). Remove the strips of orange zest and stir in the chocolate until it has completely melted, then the candied orange peel, if using.

Spoon into 4 small warm bowls or cups and set a cinnamon stick and a slice of candied peel in each one. Sprinkle with icing sugar and serve immediately with pouring cream.

This is truly outrageous, and all the better for it! It's probably the most decadent version of classic bread and butter pudding there is, and it is equally at home both as an informal indulgence and as a real dinner party treat. Try using the best *pains au chocolat* you can find, preferably the ones with twin chocolate bars inside. This recipe will even transform the soft supermarket variety into something sublime!

pain au chocolat pudding

4 large *pains au chocolat* (preferably with twin chocolate bars in each)

300 ml milk

300 ml double cream

1 vanilla pod, split lengthways

4 egg yolks

125 g golden caster sugar

100 g dark chocolate (60–70% cocoa solids), grated (or even chocolate chips)

icing sugar, to dust

pouring cream, to serve

a 1.7-litre shallow baking dish, greased

a large roasting tin

SERVES 6

Cut the *pains au chocolat* into thick slices. Arrange the slices, cut-side up and overlapping, in the prepared baking dish.

Put the milk, cream and vanilla pod in a pan. Cook over very low heat for about 5 minutes, or until the mixture is almost boiling and well flavoured with aromatic vanilla. Remove from the heat.

Preheat the oven to 180°C (350°F) Gas 4.

In a large bowl, whisk together the egg yolks and caster sugar until light and creamy. Strain the flavoured milk through a sieve into the egg mixture, whisking well. Whisk in 75 g of the chocolate. Pour the egg mixture evenly over the *pains au chocolat* and leave to stand for 10 minutes to allow them to absorb the liquid.

Sprinkle over the remaining chocolate. Put the baking dish in a large roasting tin and pour in enough boiling water to come halfway up the sides of the dish. Bake the pudding for 40–45 minutes, or until the custard is softly set and the top is crisp and golden brown.

Remove from the oven, lift out of the roasting tin and set aside until just warm. Sprinkle with the icing sugar and serve with cream.

This deliciously gooey brownie pudding is an ideal recipe for absolute beginners. If you have suitable oven to tableware it can be made, baked and served in the same dish so it's a treat for chocolate lovers and washer-uppers alike!

brownie lava pudding

50 g pecan pieces

100 g good-quality dark chocolate

115 g unsalted butter, cubed

175 g caster sugar

2 large eggs, lightly beaten

¼ teaspoon vanilla extract

75 g plain flour

pouring cream or vanilla ice cream, to serve

a flameproof, ovenproof baking dish, approximately 18 cm (across top) and 7 cm deep

SERVES 4–6

Preheat the oven to 180°C (350°F) Gas 4. Put the pecan pieces into a baking dish and lightly toast in the preheated oven for about 10 minutes. Leave to cool.

Meanwhile break up the chocolate and put it in the flameproof, ovenproof baking dish (or in a medium-sized saucepan). Add the butter and melt gently over very, very low heat, stirring frequently.

Remove from the heat and stir in the sugar, then gradually stir in the eggs followed by the vanilla extract.

When thoroughly mixed, stir in the flour, then finally the nuts. When there are no more floury streaks, scrape down the sides of the dish (if using) so that the mixture doesn't scorch, and put the dish into the preheated oven. Alternatively, if using a pan, transfer the mixture to a greased ovenproof dish.

Bake in the preheated oven for about 30 minutes until the mixture is set on top with a soft gooey layer at the bottom.

Serve immediately with pouring cream or vanilla ice cream on the side.

upside-down fruit pudding

A sophisticated-looking pudding that is really easy to make. Any fresh, ripe fruit can
be used, but pears are particularly good.

3 pears, peeled, cored and halved

100 g butter, softened

100 g golden caster sugar

40 g ground almonds

2 eggs

100 g self-raising flour

30 g unsweetened cocoa powder

1 teaspoon baking powder

75 ml milk

icing sugar, to dust

clotted cream, to serve

a loose-bottomed flan tin,
25 cm in diameter, greased

SERVES 6

Preheat the oven to 180°C (350°F) Gas 4.

Arrange the pears in the bottom of the prepared flan tin. Put the butter
and sugar in a bowl and cream until smooth. Add the ground almonds
and eggs and beat well. Sift in the flour, cocoa and baking powder,
then fold the mixture together. Add the milk and mix until smooth.
Cover the pears with the mixture, smoothing it out with a palette
knife. Bake in the preheated oven for 25 minutes.

Remove from the oven, leave to cool for 10 minutes, then turn out
onto a plate. Remove the outer ring of the flan tin, and lift off the base
by sliding a palette knife underneath it. Dust the pudding with icing
sugar and serve with clotted cream.

There is nothing better on a cold winter's day than a steamed pudding waiting to be turned out and smothered in custard. This pudding looks good enough to serve at a dinner party. Smaller oranges are best here, and don't peel them – they are cooked, skins and all, for maximum effect.

chocolate, orange and date steamed pudding

100 g golden caster sugar

2–3 seedless oranges

200 g unsalted butter, softened

200 g dark muscovado sugar

finely grated zest of
1 unwaxed orange

3 tablespoons fine-cut
orange marmalade

3 eggs, beaten

1 tablespoon orange-flower water
(optional)

150 g plain flour

50 g unsweetened cocoa powder

2 teaspoons baking powder

150 g ready-to-eat dates, chopped

Crème Anglaise (page 145) or
Chocolate Custard Sauce
(page 147), to serve

a 1.2-litre pudding basin, greased

SERVES 6–8

First make a sugar syrup. Pour 150 ml water into a small saucepan and add the caster sugar. Cook over gentle heat until dissolved.

Slice each orange thinly into about 6 neat slices. Submerge them in the sugar syrup. Set a disc of non-stick greaseproof paper on top and simmer gently for 30–40 minutes. Lift the oranges out with a slotted spoon and drain on a wire rack. Boil the syrup until reduced by half.

Line the base of the pudding basin with a disc of non-stick greaseproof paper. Place the best orange slice on top of the disc, and use the rest of the slices to line the sides of the basin.

In a large bowl, cream the butter, muscovado sugar and orange zest using an electric whisk, until light and fluffy. Beat in the marmalade, then gradually beat in the eggs and orange-flower water, if using, mixing well between each addition. Sift the flour, cocoa and baking powder into the egg mixture and fold in. Finally, fold in the dates.

Spoon the mixture into the basin. It should come about three-quarters of the way up the sides. Smooth the surface and cover with a disc of non-stick greaseproof paper. Take a large sheet of aluminium foil and fold it in half. Make a pleat in the centre and place over the basin with the pleat in the centre. Press the foil over the side of the basin, tie around the top with string and trim away any excess foil. The pleat will open out and allow the pudding to expand during cooking. Stand the basin on a trivet in a large, deep pan and add enough water to come at least 5 cm up the sides. Cover with a lid and simmer gently for 2 hours, topping up the water level from time to time.

Remove the foil and disc and insert a skewer into the centre of the pudding. If it doesn't come out clean, re-cover and steam for a little longer. Run a knife around the sides, turn out onto a dish and brush with syrup. Serve with Crème Anglaise or Chocolate Custard Sauce.

hot jamaican chocolate bananas

These are a favourite with adults and children, but just leave out the rum if you are serving these to kids. They are really easy to make and can be cooked on the barbecue, too, so they make a great sweet treat for both winter and summer.

4 firm bananas, peeled

50 ml rum (optional)

100 g dark chocolate, grated

16 raspberries, to serve

100 g vanilla ice cream
or frozen yoghurt

SERVES 4

Preheat the oven to 190°C (375°F) Gas 5.

Put each banana on a square of aluminium foil. Pour over the rum, if using, and wrap up to make a parcel. Put the parcels on a baking tray and bake in the centre of the preheated oven for 5 minutes.

Put the chocolate in a small, heatproof bowl set over a small saucepan of steaming but not boiling water and melt gently (do not let the base of the bowl touch the water). Stir occasionally, until smooth.

Remove the bananas from the oven, carefully unwrap the foil parcels and transfer the bananas to a serving plate or bowl. Add 4 raspberries to each plate, then drizzle the melted chocolate over. Serve immediately with a scoop of ice cream or frozen yoghurt.

This is a very simple idea for creating a marvellous special occasion pudding.
Buy the chocolate you most like to eat (there is a huge variety of brands and types available).
Use small saucepans or pretty heatproof bowls set on the table over a warming tray or three
candle-warmers – and have lots of fun.

chocolate fondue

100 g dark chocolate, chopped

100 g white chocolate, chopped

100 g milk chocolate, chopped

9 tablespoons double cream

1 tablespoon Bacardi rum
or Grand Marnier (optional)

to serve

1 small pineapple

2 bananas

125 g strawberries

125 g cherries

2 medium pears

*a fondue set, small saucepans
or heatproof bowls*

SERVES 4–6

Put each type of chocolate into separate small, heatproof bowls set over small saucepans of steaming but not boiling water and melt gently (do not let the base of the bowls touch the water). Stir occasionally, until smooth. Remove the bowls from the heat.

Put the cream into a separate saucepan, bring to the boil, then add 3 tablespoons to each saucepan or bowl of melted chocolate and mix gently. If using Bacardi or Grand Marnier, add it to the white chocolate mixture.

Set the bowls over the lowest possible heat on a warming tray in the centre of the table, surrounded by the fruit. Cut the fruit at the table and immediately dip into the melted chocolate fondues and eat.

These delicious soufflés, with their exceedingly light and meltingly soft texture, are more like hot chocolate mousses. The recipe is easy though – if you can make meringue you can make these soufflés. Serve with crisp biscuits for a stunning finale to a special meal.

chocolate soufflés

about 1 tablespoon melted butter

180 g dark chocolate, chopped

150 ml double cream

3 large eggs, separated

2 tablespoons Cognac or brandy

2 large egg whites

3 tablespoons caster sugar,
plus extra for the soufflé dishes

icing sugar, to dust

*4 soufflé dishes, 300 ml each,
or 4 large coffee cups*

SERVES 4

Brush the soufflé dishes with the melted butter, then sprinkle with sugar to give an even coating. Stand the dishes on a baking tray or in a roasting tin.

Put the chocolate into a medium, heavy-based saucepan, pour in the cream, then set over very low heat and stir frequently until melted and smooth. Remove from the heat and stir in the egg yolks, one at a time, followed by the Cognac or brandy. At this point the mixture can be covered and set aside for up to 2 hours.

Preheat the oven to 220°C (425°F) Gas 7.

Put the 5 egg whites into a spotlessly clean, grease-free bowl and, using an electric whisk, whisk until stiff peaks form. Gradually whisk in the caster sugar to give a glossy, stiff meringue. The chocolate mixture should feel comfortably warm to your finger, so gently reheat if necessary. Using a large metal spoon, add a little of the meringue to the chocolate mixture and mix thoroughly. This loosens the consistency, making it easier to incorporate the rest of the meringue. Pour the chocolate mixture on top of the remaining meringue and gently fold both mixtures together until just blended.

Spoon the mixture into the prepared soufflé dishes – the mixture should come to just below the rims. Bake in the preheated oven for 8–10 minutes until barely set – the centres should be soft and wobble when gently shaken. Dust with icing sugar and eat immediately.

little hot chocolate mousses

The point of these wonderful puddings is that the centre is still blissfully liquid when you serve them, so don't be tempted to cook them for any longer than the stated time. They are delicious served on their own or with ice cream.

5 eggs, plus 5 egg yolks

115 g caster sugar

225 g dark chocolate (60–70% cocoa solids), finely chopped

200 g unsalted butter

75 g plain flour

50 g unsweetened cocoa powder, plus extra to dust

ice cream, to serve (optional)

8 ramekins, greased, or non-stick dariole moulds

SERVES 8

Preheat the oven to 180°C (350°F) Gas 4.

Put the eggs, egg yolks and sugar in a large bowl and beat with an electric whisk until the mixture is pale yellow, 10–15 minutes.

Put the chocolate and butter in a heatproof bowl set over a small saucepan of steaming but not boiling water and melt gently (do not let the base of the bowl touch the water). Stir occasionally, until smooth. Remove the bowl from the heat. Add a small amount of the egg and sugar mixture to the melted chocolate and stir until well mixed. Add the rest of the egg mixture and mix well. Sift the flour and cocoa powder into the bowl and gently fold it in with a large metal spoon until just mixed.

Stand the prepared ramekins or moulds in a roasting tin and spoon the mixture into them (the mixture should come to just below the rims). Bake on the middle shelf of the preheated oven for 10–12 minutes until risen and just firm to the touch. Don't cook them any longer than this or they will set inside.

Run a round-bladed knife around the inside of each mould to loosen the puddings, then carefully turn them out onto individual plates. Dust with cocoa powder and serve immediately, either on their own or with your favourite ice cream.

An individual white chocolate sponge pudding, baked with a hidden centre of molten chocolate and served with cream or Chocolate Fudge Sauce (page 150), is perfect for any occasion. It is very important to use the best-quality white and dark chocolate you can find.

white and black puddings

cream or Chocolate Fudge Sauce
(page 150) (optional)

dark chocolate filling

75 g dark chocolate, chopped

80 ml double cream

white chocolate sponge

100 g white chocolate, chopped

175 g unsalted butter,
at room temperature

150 g golden caster sugar

3 large eggs, beaten

250 g self-raising flour

a pinch of salt

½ teaspoon vanilla extract

about 4 tablespoons milk

an ice cube tray, oiled

*6 small pudding moulds,
7.5 cm in diameter, well greased*

SERVES 6

The dark chocolate filling should be made at least 1 hour before making the sponge (though the filling can be kept in the freezer for up to 1 week). Put the chocolate into a heatproof bowl set over a saucepan of steaming but not boiling water and melt gently (do not let the base of the bowl touch the water). Stir occasionally, until smooth. Remove the bowl from the heat, stir in the cream, then pour into the prepared ice cube tray to make 6 'cubes'. Freeze for at least 1 hour.

Preheat the oven to 180°C (350°F) Gas 4.

When ready to make the pudding, put the white chocolate in a heatproof bowl set over a saucepan of steaming but not boiling water and melt gently (do not let the base of the bowl touch the water). Stir occasionally, until smooth. Remove from the heat, then leave to cool.

Put the butter into a large bowl and, using a wooden spoon or electric mixer, beat the butter until creamy, then gradually beat in the sugar. When the mixture is very light and fluffy, beat in the eggs, 1 tablespoon at a time, beating well after each addition. Using a large metal spoon, carefully fold in the flour and salt, followed by the melted chocolate, vanilla extract and just enough milk to give the mixture a firm dropping consistency. Spoon the mixture into the prepared moulds to fill by about half. Turn out the dark chocolate cubes, put one into the centre of each mould, then top up with more sponge mixture so each one is three-quarters full.

Stand the moulds in a roasting tin, then cover loosely with well-buttered foil. Bake in the preheated oven for about 25 minutes or until just firm to the touch. Run a round-bladed knife inside each mould to loosen the puddings, then carefully turn out onto plates. Serve with cream or Chocolate Fudge Sauce, if using.

nutella and bananas on brioche

Children (and adults) around the world are grateful for one of Italy's biggest exports – Nutella. This luxurious chocolate spread made with hazelnuts and chocolate is marvellous just scooped up and devoured by the spoonful. But when warmed up between two pieces of brioche with some banana it becomes something sublime!

4 thick slices of brioche bread

4 tablespoons Nutella or other chocolate-hazelnut spread

1 small banana, peeled and thinly sliced

vegetable oil, for brushing

a panini press

SERVES 2

Preheat the panini press.

Spread 2 slices of the brioche with the Nutella. Place the banana slices on top. Close the sandwiches with the second slice of brioche. Brush both sides of the panini with a little oil and toast in the preheated panini press for 2 minutes, or according to the manufacturer's instructions. The bread should be golden brown and the filling warmed through.

chilled desserts

This amazingly popular pudding is said to have originated in Venice in the 1950s, and it is one that benefits from being made the day before. For added texture, grind real chocolate in a blender for layering and sprinkling. Make this in a large glass dish or in individual glasses for a special occasion.

tiramisù with raspberries

150 g dark chocolate, (60–70% cocoa solids)

300 ml double cream

100 ml freshly brewed Italian espresso

6 tablespoons Marsala wine

250 g mascarpone cheese

5 tablespoons caster sugar

2 tablespoons dark rum

2 egg yolks

24 *savoiardi* biscuits

200 g raspberries, plus extra to serve

a serving dish or 4 glasses

SERVES 4 GENEROUSLY

Put the chocolate in a food processor and grind to a powder. Set aside. Pour the cream into a bowl and whisk until soft peaks form. Set aside. Pour the espresso into a second bowl and stir in 2 tablespoons of the Marsala. Set aside. Put the mascarpone in a third bowl and whisk in 3 tablespoons of the sugar, then beat in 2 tablespoons of the Marsala and the rum. Set aside.

To make a zabaglione mixture, put the egg yolks, 2 tablespoons Marsala and the remaining 2 tablespoons sugar in a medium heatproof bowl and beat with an electric whisk until well blended. Set over a saucepan of steaming but not boiling water (do not let the base of the bowl touch the water). Whisk the mixture until it is glossy, pale, light and fluffy and holds a trail when dropped from the whisk. This should take about 5 minutes. Remove from the heat and whisk until cold. Fold in the whipped cream, then fold in the mascarpone mixture.

Dip the *savoiardi*, one at a time, into the espresso mixture. Do not leave them in for too long or they will disintegrate. Start assembling the tiramisù by arranging half the dipped *savoiardi* in the bottom of a serving dish or 4 glasses. Trickle over some of the leftover espresso. Add a layer of raspberries.

Sprinkle with one-third of the ground chocolate, then add half the zabaglione-cream-mascarpone mixture. Arrange the remaining *savoiardi* on top, moisten with any remaining espresso, add some more raspberries and sprinkle with half the remaining chocolate. Finally spoon over the remaining zabaglione-cream-mascarpone and finish with a thick layer of chocolate and extra raspberries. Chill in the refrigerator for at least 3 hours (overnight is better) for the flavours to develop. Serve chilled.

In these magnificent ice-cream creations, hot fudge sauce contrasts with chilly ice cream and bananas. If that wasn't enough, whipped cream, toasted nuts and a cherry top everything off for a sinful splurge.

banana splits with hot fudge sauce

4 small bananas, peeled

4 scoops each of strawberry, vanilla and chocolate ice cream

4 maraschino cherries

60 g shelled pecan nuts, chopped and toasted

hot fudge sauce

90 g dark chocolate, chopped

175 ml double cream

2 tablespoons butter

75 ml golden syrup

1 teaspoon vanilla extract

100 g caster sugar

whipped cream

250 ml double cream

1 tablespoon caster sugar

1 teaspoon vanilla extract

4 shallow pudding bowls

SERVES 4

To make the hot fudge sauce, put the chocolate, cream and butter in a medium saucepan. When melted, add the golden syrup, vanilla extract and sugar, stirring constantly over medium heat. When nearly boiling, turn the heat down to low and simmer for 15 minutes without stirring. Leave to cool for 5 minutes before using.

To make the whipped cream, whisk the double cream with the sugar and vanilla extract and set aside. Cut the bananas in half lengthways. Take the pudding bowls and put 2 banana halves along the sides of each one. Put one scoop of each flavour of ice cream between the bananas. Top with one spoonful of the whipped cream, a sprinkling of pecan nuts and a cherry on top. Serve with a small jug of the hot fudge sauce to pour over.

These decadent profiteroles contain a surprise (*sorpresa*) inside: little balls of chocolatey, hazelnutty semifreddo, a kind of ice cream which stays soft when frozen.

profiteroles con sorpresa

Hot Fudge Sauce (page 39, but omitting the golden syrup), to serve

gianduja semifreddo

125 g skinned toasted hazelnuts

125 g dark chocolate (60–70% cocoa solids), chopped

600 ml double cream

2 eggs, separated

175 g icing sugar

choux pastry

80 g unsalted butter, cubed

100 g plain flour, sifted twice with a pinch of salt

2–3 eggs, beaten

a 1.25-litre freezerproof container

3 baking trays, lined with non-stick baking parchment

SERVES 6

To make the semifreddo, grind the nuts very finely. Put the chocolate into a heatproof bowl set over a saucepan of steaming water and melt gently (do not let the base of the bowl touch the water). Remove the bowl from the heat and stir until just smooth. Put the cream in a bowl and whisk until soft peaks form, then fold in the ground nuts. Put the egg yolks in another bowl with 2 tablespoons of the sugar and whisk until pale and creamy. Put the egg whites in a spotlessly clean, grease-free bowl and whisk until soft peaks form. Add the remaining sugar to the whites, spoonful by spoonful, whisking between each addition, until very thick. Stir the chocolate into the egg yolk mixture. Fold in the cream, then the meringue mixture. Spoon into a freezer container. Freeze for 12 hours until firm. Put a lined baking tray in the freezer. Take the semifreddo out of the freezer and refrigerate for 10 minutes before scooping into small balls with an ice cream scoop and spacing apart on the frozen baking tray. Freeze until hard.

Preheat the oven to 200°C (400°F) Gas 6.

To make the choux pastry, put the butter and 200 ml water in a heavy saucepan and bring slowly to the boil until the butter has completely melted. As soon as it hits a rolling boil, add all the flour, remove the pan from the heat and beat with a wooden spoon. It is ready when the mixture leaves the sides of the pan. Leave to cool slightly, then beat in the eggs, a little at a time, until the mixture is very smooth and shiny. If the eggs are large, it may not be necessary to add all of them. The mixture should just flop off the spoon when you bang it on the side of the pan. Space teaspoons of the mixture apart on the baking trays and bake in the preheated oven for 20–30 minutes, or until deep golden.

Remove from the oven and split each one almost in two. Return to the oven for 5 minutes. Cool on a wire rack. Put a semifreddo ball in each one, pushing the halves almost together. Pile into a dish and refrigerate for 10 minutes, then pour over the Hot Fudge Sauce and serve.

A truly seductive end to any party, these fruits make for a great finale.
Super easy to make, but remember to make them at least 1 hour in advance.

strawberries and cherries
in tricolour chocolate

250 g strawberries, stalks on

250 g cherries, stalks on

30 g milk chocolate, chopped

30 g white chocolate, chopped

30 g dark chocolate, chopped

SERVES 4

Divide the strawberries and cherries into 3 equal piles.

Put the milk chocolate in a heatproof bowl set over a small saucepan of steaming but not boiling water and melt gently (do not let the base of the bowl touch the water). Stir occasionally, until smooth, then remove the bowl from the heat.

Take one of the piles of fruit and dip them halfway into the chocolate, leaving the tops and stalks uncoated and visible. Transfer to a sheet of greaseproof paper to set.

Repeat with the white and dark chocolate and the other 2 piles of fruit. Refrigerate for at least 1 hour.

To serve, peel off the greaseproof paper and pile the fruit onto a large serving plate.

very rich chocolate brûlées

The smooth chocolate cream in these brûlées can be made up to 2 days ahead, with the crunchy caramel topping added just before serving. You need a really hot grill or a cook's blowtorch, available from kitchen suppliers for the best mirror-like finish. If you like, the vanilla pod can be replaced with 1 tablespoon dark rum, added to the mixture at the same time as the egg yolks.

600 ml double cream

1 vanilla pod, split lengthways

300 g dark chocolate, chopped

4 large egg yolks

60 g icing sugar, sifted

about 4 tablespoons caster sugar, to sprinkle

8 small soufflé dishes or ramekins, 150 ml each

SERVES 8

Pour the cream into a heavy-based saucepan and add the vanilla pod. Heat gently until just too hot for your finger to bear. Cover with a lid and leave to infuse for about 30 minutes.

Preheat the oven to 180°C (350°F) Gas 4.

Lift out the vanilla pod and, using a tip of a knife, scrape the seeds into the cream. Gently reheat the cream, then remove from the heat and stir in the chocolate. When melted and smooth, leave to cool until just warm.

Meanwhile, put the egg yolks and icing sugar into a mixing bowl, beat with a wooden spoon until well blended, then stir in the warm chocolate cream. Pour into the soufflé dishes, then stand the dishes in a roasting tin half-filled with warm water. Cook in the preheated oven for about 30 minutes until just firm. Remove from the roasting tin and leave to cool, then cover and chill overnight or for up to 48 hours.

When ready to serve, preheat the grill to maximum and half-fill the roasting tin with ice cubes and water. Sprinkle the tops of the chocolate creams with caster sugar, then set the soufflé dishes in the icy water (this prevents the chocolate melting) and quickly flash under the grill or with a blowtorch until the sugar melts and caramelizes. Eat within 1 hour.

white chocolate and raspberry fools

This is a pretty marbled dessert with a luxurious hint of white chocolate –
an ideal quick and indulgent treat after a light evening meal.

40 g white chocolate, chopped

125 g raspberries

200 g fromage frais

SERVES 2

Put the chocolate in a heatproof bowl set over a small saucepan of steaming but not boiling water and melt gently (do not let the base of the bowl touch the water). Stir occasionally, until smooth, then remove the bowl from the heat.

Reserve 6 raspberries to decorate, then roughly crush the remaining raspberries with a fork.

Mix the fromage frais into the melted chocolate, then gently fold in the crushed raspberries to give a marbled effect. Spoon into 2 glasses and decorate with the reserved raspberries. Cover and refrigerate until ready to serve.

This is the sort of dessert French aunties would have made in the kitchen of their country house during the summer holidays. And most respectable aunties would have had special little pots, about the size of espresso cups, solely for this purpose. You can also use regular crème brûlée ramekins. Good-quality chocolate is imperative.

chocolate cream pots

250 ml whole milk

250 ml double cream

100 g dark chocolate (at least 70% cocoa solids), finely chopped

3 large whole eggs and 2 egg yolks

125 g caster sugar

6 ramekins or other heatproof containers

a baking dish

SERVES 6

Put the milk and cream in a saucepan. Bring just to the boil and remove from the heat. Stir in the chocolate until melted.

Put the eggs, yolks and sugar in a large bowl and mix well, but don't whisk until frothy; the finished dish should be smooth on top and whisking too much will make too many bubbles that mar the surface. Pour in the milk mixture and stir gently until just mixed.

Bring a kettle of water to the boil and preheat the oven to 180°C (350°F) Gas 4.

Set the ramekins in the baking dish. Ladle the chocolate mixture into each ramekin to fill well. Open the preheated oven, pull out the shelf and set the baking dish with the ramekins on the shelf. Pour the boiling water into the baking dish to come about two-thirds up the sides of the ramekins. Carefully push the shelf back in.

Cook until just set and still a bit jiggly in the middle, 25–30 minutes. Remove the dish from the oven, leave to stand for 5 minutes, then remove the ramekins from the water bath. Leave to cool uncovered. Serve warm or at room temperature.

This is a great dessert to make when you've got some cranberries stashed in the freezer or during the Christmas season when they are fresh. Their fruity sharpness beautifully complements the chocolate. The result is a tempting, deep red compote hidden under a layer of darkest chocolate mousse. This is for adults only!

dracula's delight

cranberry compote

150 g fresh or frozen cranberries

75 g golden caster sugar

2 tablespoons Cointreau

chocolate mousse

200 g dark chocolate (60–70% cocoa solids), chopped

3 tablespoons freshly brewed strong espresso

25 g unsalted butter, cubed

1½ tablespoons chocolate liqueur

3 large eggs, separated

4 deep glasses or pots

SERVES 4

To make the cranberry compote, put the cranberries in a small pan with a splash of water and the sugar. Bring to the boil and simmer for 5 minutes until all the cranberries have burst and the compote is thick. Stir in the Cointreau, then spoon into the glasses. Leave to cool.

To make the chocolate mousse, put the chocolate, espresso and butter in a heatproof bowl set over a small saucepan of steaming but not boiling water and melt gently (do not let the base of the bowl touch the water). Stir occasionally, until smooth, then remove the bowl from the heat. Stir in the liqueur. Stir in the egg yolks while the chocolate mixture is still hot – this will cook them slightly.

Using an electric whisk, whisk the egg whites in a spotlessly clean, grease-free bowl until they form firm peaks. Using a metal spoon, stir a large spoonful of egg whites into the chocolate mixture to loosen it, then gently fold in the rest. Spoon the mousse on top of the cranberry compote. Cover and refrigerate for at least 6 hours or overnight.

For a dinner party, put the fresh raspberry purée in the bottom of attractive wine glasses and pipe the mousse over the top.

white chocolate mousses

125 g best-quality white chocolate, chopped, plus 15 g, finely grated

1½ leaves of gelatine

60 g caster sugar

2 egg whites

1 teaspoon Framboise (optional)

300 ml whipping cream, whisked until it starts to thicken

raspberry purée

400 g raspberries

icing sugar, to taste

6–8 wine glasses or glass dishes

a non-stick baking tray

SERVES 6–8

Preheat the oven to 160°C (325°F) Gas 3.

To make the raspberry purée, put the raspberries in a blender, with icing sugar to taste, and whizz until smooth. If you prefer a smooth result, push the raspberry purée through a fine-mesh nylon sieve to remove the seeds. Divide the purée among the glass dishes.

Put the chocolate in a heatproof bowl set over a small saucepan of steaming but not boiling water and melt gently (do not let the base of the bowl touch the water). Stir occasionally, until smooth. Remove the bowl from the heat and leave to cool.

Put the gelatine in a small saucepan and cover with cold water. Leave to soak for 3 minutes until soft, then drain off the water.

Meanwhile, put the sugar on a non-stick baking tray and heat in the preheated oven for 5 minutes. Put the egg whites and half the warm sugar in a large bowl and whisk with an electric whisk until stiff peaks form. Beat in the remaining sugar until the mixture is shiny and smooth. Whisk in the Framboise, if using.

Heat the softened gelatine over very low heat, swirling the pan, until it dissolves. Add it to the meringue and stir gently with a large metal spoon to mix. Gently fold in the cooled chocolate, then fold in the whisked cream until the mixture is smooth. Finally, stir in the grated chocolate.

Spoon the mousse on top of the puréed fruit. Alternatively, for a special occasion, pipe the mixture from a large piping bag fitted with a wide, plain nozzle. Refrigerate for at least 30 minutes before serving.

These white chocolate cases are a bit fiddly to make, but the end result of these creamy, luscious mousses is so divine that it's worth every minute of preparation. They are quite rich, so serve them to guests with a cup of espresso at the end of a light meal.

dark chocolate, prune and armagnac mousses

140 g white chocolate, melted and slightly cooled, plus extra shavings to decorate

5 ready-to-eat prunes, stoned

1 tablespoon Armagnac

60 g dark chocolate (70–80% cocoa solids)

½ tablespoon butter

1½ tablespoons double cream

1 egg, separated

frosted edible flower petals, to decorate (optional)

a thin sheet of perspex

sticky tape

a baking tray, lined with greaseproof paper

MAKES 8

Cut out eight 4 x 15-cm strips of perspex, coil each one to make a collar, about 4 cm in diameter, and secure with sticky tape. Stand the collars on the prepared baking tray.

Using a teaspoon, coat the inside of each collar with the white chocolate, leaving the top ragged and smeared. Drop a spoonful of chocolate into the bottom of each collar and spread out to form a base. Chill for about 15 minutes, then remove from the refrigerator and add a little more chocolate to any thin patches so that there's a good layer of chocolate all round. Return to the refrigerator and chill for at least 30 minutes.

Put the prunes, Armagnac and 2 tablespoons water in a food processor and blend to make a smooth purée. Put the dark chocolate in a heatproof bowl set over a small saucepan of steaming but not boiling water and melt gently (do not let the base of the bowl touch the water). Stir occasionally, until smooth. Remove from the heat and stir in the butter until melted, then stir in the prune purée, cream and egg yolk.

Put the egg white in a spotlessly clean, grease-free bowl and whisk to form stiff peaks. Fold a spoonful into the chocolate mixture, then fold in the remaining egg white, one-third at a time. Carefully spoon about 2 tablespoons of the mousse into the white chocolate cases and refrigerate for at least 2 hours.

To serve, carefully remove the sticky tape and unpeel the perspex collars. Arrange on a serving plate using a spatula and decorate with shavings of white chocolate or frosted edible flower petals, if liked.

For a silky smooth texture, make sure the chocolate, gelatine and egg yolk mixture
is still warm when folded together, before adding the cream.

chocolate marquise

250 g dark couverture chocolate
(70% cocoa solids), chopped

3 leaves of gelatine

3 egg yolks

25 g caster sugar

2 tablespoons brandy (optional)

400 ml whipping cream

unsweetened cocoa powder,
to dust

single cream, to serve

a sugar thermometer

*a non-stick loaf tin, 500 g, greased
and lined with 2 long strips of non-
stick greaseproof paper so the ends
hang over the 4 edges of the tin*

SERVES 6

Put the chocolate in a heatproof bowl set over a small saucepan of
steaming but not boiling water and melt gently (do not let the base of
the bowl touch the water). Stir occasionally, until smooth. Remove the
bowl from the heat and leave to cool slightly.

Put the gelatine in a small saucepan and cover with cold water. Leave to
soak for 3 minutes until soft, then drain off the water. Heat the gelatine
over very low heat, swirling the pan, until the gelatine dissolves.

Put the egg yolks in a large, heatproof bowl and beat with an electric
whisk until pale and creamy.

Put the sugar and 50 ml water in a small saucepan and heat gently
until the sugar has dissolved. Increase the heat and cook for 3 minutes
or until the temperature of the water has reached 118°C/240°F –
check with a sugar thermometer. Gently pour the sugar syrup onto the
egg yolks, beating with an electric whisk as you pour, until the mixture
becomes thick and creamy. Beat in the brandy, if using. Add half the
warm chocolate and stir well with a large metal spoon until well
mixed. Gently stir in the remaining chocolate, followed by the warm
gelatine solution.

Put the cream in a bowl and whisk until it starts to thicken. Using a
large metal spoon, gently fold the cream into the chocolate mixture.
Pour the mixture into the prepared loaf tin, tapping the base gently on
the work surface so the mixture reaches the corners. Level the top with
a knife. Cover and chill overnight in the refrigerator until set.

When ready to serve, gently lift the marquise out of the tin by pulling
up on the greaseproof paper and transfer to a serving plate. Dust with
cocoa powder, then cut into thick slices. Serve with a drizzle of cream.

chocolate, coffee and vanilla bombe

This impressive recipe is for a single, large bombe, but you can just as easily use individual dariole moulds instead.

4 egg yolks

2 teaspoons cornflour

75 g caster sugar

300 ml milk

5 tablespoons freshly brewed espresso

1 teaspoon vanilla extract

300 ml whipping cream

100 g dark chocolate, chopped

chocolate shavings, to serve

3 freezerproof containers

a 750-ml mould or pudding basin

SERVES 4–6

Whisk together the egg yolks, cornflour and sugar until smooth and creamy. Heat the milk in a pan until almost boiling, then gradually whisk into the egg mixture until smooth. Return to the pan and heat very gently, stirring, for 5–10 minutes until you get a thick custard. Pour into a bowl, press clingfilm onto the surface and leave to cool, then refrigerate.

Divide the custard between 3 bowls. Stir the espresso into one and the vanilla extract into another. Whip the cream until thick and just holding in soft peaks, then fold one-third into the coffee custard and one-third into the vanilla custard.

Put the chocolate in a heatproof bowl set over a small saucepan of steaming but not boiling water and melt gently (do not let the base of the bowl touch the water). Stir occasionally, until smooth. Fold into the third bowl of custard. Fold in a little cream to loosen the mixture, then fold in the remaining cream.

Transfer the 3 custards into the individual freezerproof containers and freeze for about 1 hour until beginning to set around the sides. Blend each one in a food processor and return to the freezer for another 30 minutes.

Blend the chocolate ice cream, then scoop into the mould or basin and spread out in an even layer. Cover and freeze for a further hour, then blend the coffee ice cream and spread on top of the chocolate layer. Blend the vanilla ice cream, then gently spread on top. Re-cover and freeze overnight, or until firm.

To serve, dip the mould in hot water briefly, then turn out onto a serving plate. Decorate with chocolate shavings and serve in slices.

mint chocolate chip ice cream

One for the adults, for when they're jealous of the kids' Rocky Road Ice Cream below.

1 quantity Rich Vanilla Ice Cream
(page 143)

about 100 g chocolate-covered
mints, frozen

SERVES 4–6

Put the mints in a food processor and zap to a coarse meal. Stir into freshly churned ice cream. Alternatively, churn the ice cream with half the chocolate mints, then stir in the remainder and freeze.

rocky road ice cream

One for the kids, to put a big smile on their faces.

100 g mini-marshmallows

a tub of shop-bought chocolate
ice cream, softened slightly

nut brittle

75 g sugar

50 g shelled pecan nuts or almonds,
coarsely crushed

peanut or corn oil, for brushing

SERVES 4

To make the nut brittle, put the sugar and 6 tablespoons water in a saucepan, stir well, then bring to the boil over medium heat. Continue boiling until golden brown, then add the crushed nuts. Pour onto a greased baking tray, leave to cool and set. When set, break up the brittle, then crush with a rolling pin.

Stir the nut brittle and marshmallows into the softened ice cream until evenly distributed. Freeze. Serve with extras such as chopped nuts, shaved chocolate and nut brittle.

Nobody makes pistachio ice cream like the Italians, but this home-style version is fairly authentic. Most supermarkets sell shelled unsalted pistachios – the roasted and salted snack kind aren't suitable for this recipe. Fresh nuts taste best, so use a fresh pack.

pistachio and chocolate ice cream

100 g shelled unsalted pistachios

250 ml double cream, well chilled

300 ml milk

4 large egg yolks

100 g caster sugar

85 g dark chocolate, finely chopped

an ice-cream maker or freezerproof container

SERVES 4–6

Put the pistachios and 3 tablespoons of the cream into a food processor or blender and process to a fine paste, scraping down the sides from time to time. Transfer the paste to a medium, heavy-based saucepan and stir in the milk. Heat gently until almost boiling, stirring frequently, then remove from the heat, cover and leave to infuse for 15–20 minutes.

Put the egg yolks and sugar into a bowl and mix well. Pour in the pistachio milk and stir well. Pour the mixture back into the saucepan. Stir gently over low heat until the mixture thickens – do not let it boil or it will curdle. Remove from the heat, pour into a clean jug or bowl, leave to cool, then chill thoroughly. Put in a bowl and refrigerate.

When ready to churn, put the rest of the cream into the chilled bowl and, using a whisk, whip until soft peaks form, then stir in the pistachio mixture and the chopped chocolate. Pour into an ice-cream maker and churn until frozen. Eat immediately or store in the freezer. Alternatively, put the mixture into a freezerproof container and freeze, stirring occasionally.

Italian and French *gelaterias* offer splendid, often simple flavour combinations. Chocolate and nuts are particularly delicious, especially if the chocolate is of the high-quality, bitter-sweet type. If you have a pestle and mortar, try to pound the nuts and sugar to a very smooth texture – otherwise use an electric coffee grinder or spice grinder in short bursts.

bitter chocolate and hazelnut gelato

75 g blanched hazelnuts, finely chopped

175 g vanilla sugar or caster sugar

150 ml whole milk

250 g dark chocolate (at least 70% cocoa solids), chopped

1 tablespoon glucose syrup or corn syrup

1 tablespoon chocolate or hazelnut liqueur or dark rum

400 ml double cream

crisp wafers or biscuits, to serve (optional)

an ice-cream maker or a 1-litre freezerproof container

SERVES 4–6

Put the chopped hazelnuts in a dry frying pan and dry-fry over moderate heat, stirring constantly until they darken and smell toasty, about 2–3 minutes (take care, because they burn easily). Pour out onto a plate and leave to cool.

Put the toasted hazelnuts and 4 tablespoons of the sugar in a small electric spice grinder or coffee grinder. Grind in brief bursts, to a smooth, speckly powder.

Put the milk, chocolate and remaining sugar in a saucepan over very gentle heat. Cook until the chocolate melts, stirring constantly, then add the glucose syrup and ground sugar and nuts. Remove from the heat, put the pan into a bowl of iced water and leave to cool. Stir in the liqueur and cream and cool again.

Pour the prepared mixture into the ice-cream maker and churn for 20–25 minutes or until set. Alternatively, freeze in the container, covered, for 6 hours, beating and whisking it once after 3 hours.

Serve in scoops with crisp wafers or biscuits, if using.

chocolate chip cookie ice-cream sandwiches

These wicked sandwiches are guaranteed to be a hit with children and the young-at-heart.
Perfect for a summer lunch in the garden.

75 g unsalted butter, softened

75 g caster sugar

75 g light soft brown sugar, sifted

1 large egg, beaten

½ teaspoon vanilla extract

150 g self-raising flour

25 g unsweetened cocoa powder

¼ teaspoon salt

100 g chocolate chips (dark, milk or white), or coarsely chopped chocolate

Rich Vanilla Ice Cream (page 143), for filling

several non-stick baking trays, lightly greased

MAKES ABOUT 6

Preheat the oven to 180°C (350°F) Gas 4.

Cream the butter and sugars together until pale and fluffy. Beat in the egg and vanilla extract.

Sift the flour, cocoa and salt into a bowl, then fold into the egg mixture. Fold in the chocolate chips.

Put 4 heaped tablespoons of the mixture spaced well apart on each baking tray. Press them down and spread them out using the back of a wet spoon.

Bake in the preheated oven for 12–15 minutes. Remove from the oven, leave to cool on the baking tray for 1 minute, then transfer to a wire rack. When cold, use immediately or store in an airtight container for up to 5 days.

To assemble the sandwiches, spread a thick (about 2 cm) layer of ice cream on a cookie, then press a second one on top. Repeat until all the sandwiches are made, then freeze until ready to serve.

tarts & cheesecakes

This rich, indulgent dessert is something of a show-stopper. With a simple base made from crumbled brownies, and a filling of creamy, moussey white chocolate and coffee, it couldn't be easier to make. Use plain brownies, or ones studded with walnuts.

white chocolate and kahlúa mousse torte

350 g dark chocolate brownies

200 g white chocolate, chopped

100 ml freshly brewed espresso

2 tablespoons Kahlúa or other coffee liqueur

300 ml double cream

dark chocolate curls, to decorate

a 20-cm springform cake tin, base and sides lined with greaseproof paper

SERVES 8

Reserve about 250 g of the brownies and carefully cut the remainder into 7-mm thick slices, then use to line the sides of the prepared cake tin to a height of about 3.5 cm.

Crumble the remaining brownies into smallish chunks and scatter over the base of the tin. Using your fingers, press down gently to make a firm, flat base, then set aside.

Put the white chocolate in a small, heatproof bowl set over a small saucepan of steaming but not boiling water and melt gently (do not let the base of the bowl touch the water). Stir occasionally, until smooth. Remove from the heat and stir in the espresso until smooth and creamy, then stir in the Kahlúa. Leave to cool for 10 minutes.

Whip the cream until it just stands in peaks, then fold in a couple of spoonfuls of the coffee mixture to loosen it. Continue folding in the coffee mixture a few spoonfuls at a time to make a smooth, creamy mixture. (If it becomes lumpy, break up the lumps very gently using a wire whisk.)

Pour the mixture into the tin to fill the brownie case, then cover with clingfilm and chill overnight until set.

Remove the clingfilm, carefully release the torte from the tin and peel off the greaseproof paper. Serve decorated with dark chocolate curls and cut into slices.

This is wickedly delicious. Use the darkest chocolate you can find and serve in thin slices. The filling is gooey and rich inside – delicious with a spoonful of sour cherry jam and another of crème fraîche. If you like you can spread the base of the tart with the jam before pouring in the mixture.

baked darkest chocolate mousse tart

1 recipe Pâte Sucrée (page 157)

chocolate mousse filling
400 g dark chocolate (60–70% cocoa solids), chopped
125 g unsalted butter, cubed
5 large eggs, separated
125 g caster sugar
150 ml double cream, at room temperature
3 tablespoons dark rum (optional)

to serve
icing sugar, to dust
crème fraîche, to serve

a loose-bottomed tart tin, 25 cm in diameter, 4 cm deep

baking beans

SERVES 8

Bring the pastry to room temperature. Preheat the oven to 190°C (375°F) Gas 5.

Roll out the pastry thinly on a lightly floured work surface, then use to line the tart tin. Prick the base, then chill or freeze for 15 minutes.

Line with aluminium foil and baking beans and bake blind in the preheated oven for 15 minutes. Remove the foil and beans, reduce the heat to 180°C (350°F) Gas 4 and return to the oven for 10–15 minutes to dry out and brown. Leave to cool and remove from the tin, then transfer to a serving platter.

To make the filling, put the chocolate and butter in a heatproof bowl set over a small saucepan of steaming but not boiling water and melt gently (do not let the base of the bowl touch the water). Stir occasionally, until smooth. Remove from the heat and leave to cool for a minute or so.

Put the egg yolks and sugar in a bowl and whisk with an electric whisk until pale and creamy. Stir the cream and the rum, if using, into the melted chocolate mixture, then quickly fold in the egg yolk mixture. Put the egg whites into a spotlessly clean, grease-free bowl and whisk until soft peaks form. Quickly fold into the chocolate mixture.

Pour into the tart shell and bake for 25 minutes until risen and a bit wobbly. Remove from the oven and leave to cool – the filling will sink and firm up as it cools. Dust with icing sugar, and serve at room temperature with crème fraîche.

This unusual chocolate and almond biscuit crust is the perfect foil for a sharp lemon and almond filling.

lemon and almond tart with a chocolate amaretti crust

250 g amaretti biscuits or Italian ratafias

50 g dark chocolate, grated or chopped

75 g unsalted butter, melted

lemon almond filling

4 large eggs

zest and juice from 3 unwaxed lemons

120 g sugar

120 g unsalted butter, melted

120 g ground almonds

150 g crème fraîche

a tart tin, 23 cm in diameter, 3 cm deep

SERVES 6–8

Preheat the oven to 180°C (350°F) Gas 4.

Put the amaretti biscuits in a food processor and blend until finely crushed. Add the chocolate and blend again. Pour in the melted butter and blend until well mixed and coming together.

Put the tart tin on a baking tray. Press the mixture evenly over the base and sides of the tart tin (a potato masher and the back of a small spoon will help). Bake in the preheated oven for 10 minutes. Remove from the oven and press the puffed-up crust down again.

Beat the eggs in a bowl and whisk in the lemon zest and juice, sugar, butter and almonds. Pour into the amaretti crust and bake for about 25 minutes until set and very lightly brown on top.

Leave to cool, then spread with the crème fraîche and serve in slices at room temperature.

Chocolate lovers in Italy are well served in Piedmont, in the far north-west. The capital city, Turin, is a veritable heaven-on-earth with irresistible pastry shops on every corner. One famous delight are the *gianduiotti*, chocolates made with dark chocolate and toasted hazelnuts. This *torta* also comes from Turin, but other recipes from the region are made with almonds or walnuts and flavoured with brandy, rum or grated orange zest. Use very fresh nuts for the best flavour.

italian chocolate and hazelnut torta

100 g shelled hazelnuts

100 g plain, crisp butter biscuits, such as Petit Beurre, Abernethy or Osborne

100 g dark chocolate, chopped

1 large egg plus 1 large egg yolk, both at room temperature

3 tablespoons caster sugar

75 g unsalted butter

cocoa powder, to dust

whipped cream or ice cream, to serve

a springform cake tin, 18 cm in diameter, lightly greased and base-lined with greaseproof paper

SERVES 6–8

Preheat the oven to 200°C (400°F) Gas 6.

Put the hazelnuts in an ovenproof dish or on a baking tray and toast in the preheated oven for 5 minutes or until lightly browned (watch them carefully as they will taste bitter if they become too dark). If the hazelnuts still have their papery brown skins, put them in a clean, dry tea towel, then gather up the ends and rub the nuts together to remove the skins. Leave to cool, then chop coarsely.

Put the biscuits in a food processor and work until coarse crumbs form. Alternatively, put them in a plastic bag and crush with a rolling pin.

Put the chocolate in a heatproof bowl set over a small saucepan of steaming but not boiling water and melt gently (do not let the base of the bowl touch the water). Stir occasionally, until smooth.

Meanwhile, put the whole egg, egg yolk and sugar into a bowl and, using an electric whisk, beat vigorously until the mixture is very pale, thick and mousse-like – when the whisk is lifted, a thick ribbon-like trail slowly falls back into the bowl. Heat the butter in a small, heavy-based saucepan until just bubbling. Pour the hot butter onto the mixture in a thin, steady stream while still whisking at top speed, then whisk in the melted chocolate. Using a large metal spoon, gently fold in the chopped nuts and crushed biscuits. Pour the mixture into the prepared cake tin, spreading it gently and evenly. Cover the tin with clingfilm, then chill for at least 3 hours or overnight, until firm.

To serve, unclip the tin and remove the torta. Set on a serving plate, sprinkle with cocoa and serve, well chilled, with whipped cream or ice cream. The torta is best eaten within 5 days. Do not freeze.

Bananas, caramel and chocolate are just one of the world's best combinations – and this uses a lot of bananas! Cutting them up and standing them upright gives a wonderful deep pie that looks amazing. Use nice ripe bananas here. If you want to use fewer bananas, cut them in thick diagonal slices and spread out over the base of the pan in a thinner layer.

banana and chocolate tarte tatin

100 g golden caster sugar

50 g unsalted butter

12 medium, ripe bananas

350 g all-butter puff pastry

75 g dark chocolate (60–70% cocoa solids), finely grated

whipped cream or Crème Anglaise (page 145), to serve

a flameproof cast-iron frying pan, heavy cake tin or Tatin tin, 25 cm in diameter

SERVES 8

Preheat the oven to 190°C (375°F) Gas 5.

Put the sugar and butter in the cast-iron frying pan, heavy cake tin or Tatin tin. Place over medium heat and cook, stirring every now and then, until the mixture bubbles and turns into a smooth, rich toffee. It will look very grainy to start with and the butter will look as if it has split away from the sugar, but just keep stirring and it will gradually come together. Remove from the heat.

Cut the bananas into 3 even pieces. Arrange them standing upright in the pan or tin, packing them together.

Roll out the pastry on a lightly floured surface into a rough circle about 28 cm across. Lay the pastry over the bananas and tuck the edges down into the pan to make the rim of the tart. Prick the top of the pastry here and there with a fork, then bake in the preheated oven for 35–40 minutes, or until risen and golden. Remove the pan from the oven and leave to rest for 10 minutes.

Run a sharp knife around the pastry to free the edges. Pour out any caramel liquid that has gathered in the base and reserve. Invert a serving plate over the top of the pan. Carefully turn pan and plate over together, then remove the pan. Pour over the reserved caramel sauce and immediately sprinkle with the grated chocolate and leave to melt in the residual heat. Serve cut into wedges with whipped cream or Crème Anglaise.

A very simple and elegant tart recipe. The chestnut flavour is subtle but quite pleasant, and it makes the texture much creamier and smoother. This is easily made in advance and kept in the refrigerator until needed (up to 24 hours), but do not serve it chilled; room temperature is ideal.

chocolate chestnut tart

1 recipe Sweet Rich Shortcrust Pastry (page 156)

cocoa powder, to dust

whipped cream or sweetened crème fraîche, to serve

chocolate chestnut filling

100 g dark chocolate, chopped

3 tablespoons unsalted butter

1 large egg, beaten

200 ml double cream

250 g tinned sweetened chestnut purée

a tart tin, 23–25 cm in diameter

baking beans

SERVES 8–10

Preheat the oven to 190°C (375°F) Gas 5.

Roll out the pastry dough and use to line the tart tin. Prick the base all over with a fork, then chill for 30 minutes. Line the pastry case with greaseproof paper, then fill with baking beans. Bake on a baking tray in the preheated oven for 12–15 minutes. Remove the greaseproof paper and baking beans and return the tart shell to the oven for a further 10 minutes to dry out completely. Leave to cool slightly before filling.

Reduce the oven temperature to 150°C (300°F) Gas 2.

Put the chocolate and butter in a heatproof bowl set over a small saucepan of steaming but not boiling water and melt gently (do not let the base of the bowl touch the water). Stir occasionally, until smooth.

Stir in the egg, cream and chestnut purée and mix just to blend.

Put the tart shell back on a baking tray and set this on the oven rack, partly pulled out. (If you try to fill the shell and then transfer it to the oven, it will surely spill over the edges and burn.) Pour the chocolate mixture into the tart shell and slide the oven shelf back into place.

Bake in the preheated oven until just set, 20–25 minutes. Leave to cool to room temperature before serving.

Make these for a special dessert in the summer, when strawberries are in season and at their juicy best. The tartlets beat anything you can buy from the baker or supermarket. Brushing the inside of the tartlet shells with chocolate keeps the pastry crisp and adds a new dimension to the traditional strawberry tart.

strawberry chocolate tartlets

1 recipe Sweet Rich Shortcrust Pastry (page 156)

200 g dark chocolate, chopped

mascarpone filling

250 g mascarpone cheese

2 tablespoons caster sugar

250 g fromage frais or curd cheese

rosewater or Grand Marnier, to taste

strawberry topping

12 large, ripe strawberries

redcurrant jelly, to glaze

a biscuit cutter, 10 cm in diameter

12 deep fluted tartlet or brioche tins, 8 cm in diameter

MAKES 12

Bring the pastry to room temperature. Preheat the oven to 190°C (375°F) Gas 5.

Roll out the pastry as thinly as possible on a lightly floured work surface, then cut out 12 circles with the biscuit cutter. Use to line just 6 of the tartlet tins. Trim the edges and prick the bases. Then set another tin inside each one – this will weight down the pastry while it is baking. Chill or freeze for 15 minutes. Bake blind in the preheated oven for about 10–12 minutes until golden and set. Remove the inner tins and return the tartlet cases to the oven to dry out for 5 minutes. Leave to cool, then remove from the outer tins. Repeat with the remaining pastry to make another 6 tartlets.

Put the chocolate in a heatproof bowl set over a small saucepan of steaming but not boiling water and melt gently (do not let the base of the bowl touch the water). Stir occasionally, until smooth. Sprinkle spoonfuls of melted chocolate randomly from a height onto non-stick greaseproof paper. Leave to cool until set. Using a pastry brush, brush the remaining melted chocolate over the insides of the tartlets, making sure they are completely covered. Leave to cool until set.

To make the filling, put the mascarpone and sugar in a bowl and beat until creamy, then beat in the fromage frais. Add rosewater to taste.

Spoon this mixture into the tartlets, filling well, then sit a nice fat strawberry on top. Melt the redcurrant jelly, leave to cool slightly, then brush over the strawberries and the exposed mascarpone surface. Set aside in a cool place to set.

To serve, break up the set chocolate swirls and push a shard into each tartlet. Serve immediately.

Served warm with luxuriant coffee bean sauce, this is the tart for chocolate and coffee fiends. Decadent and refined and perfect for the end of a fabulous dinner.

chocolate pecan tart with coffee bean sauce

1 recipe Pâte Sucrée (page 157)

1 egg, beaten, to glaze

cream (optional), to serve

coffee bean sauce

1 vanilla pod, split lengthways

300 ml milk

1 tablespoon finely ground espresso coffee powder

1 tablespoon caster sugar

2 egg yolks

2 tablespoons cognac or Armagnac

chocolate filling

120 g dark chocolate (60–70% cocoa solids), chopped

50 g unsalted butter

3 large eggs, beaten

175 ml maple syrup

250 g shelled pecan nuts

a tart tin, 23 cm in diameter

baking beans

SERVES 6

To make the coffee bean sauce, put the vanilla pod, milk, coffee and sugar in a saucepan and heat gently. Bring almost to the boil, then set aside to infuse for 15 minutes. Remove the vanilla pod.

Put the egg yolks in a bowl, beat well, then pour the infused milk into the eggs. Mix well and return to the milk pan. Stir with a wooden spoon over gentle heat. When the mixture has thickened so it coats the back of the spoon, pour into a cold bowl and stir in the cognac. Cover with clingfilm, leave to cool and chill until needed.

Bring the pastry to room temperature. Preheat the oven to 190°C (375°F) Gas 5.

Roll out the pastry thinly on a lightly floured work surface, then use to line the tart tin. Prick the base, then chill or freeze for 15 minutes. Line with aluminium foil and baking beans and bake blind for 15 minutes. Remove the foil and beans, reduce the oven temperature to 180°C (350°F) Gas 4 and return to the oven for 10–15 minutes to dry out and brown. Glaze with the beaten egg and return to the oven for 5–10 minutes. Leave to cool.

Reduce the oven temperature to 160°C (325°F) Gas 3. To make the chocolate filling, put the chocolate and butter in a heatproof bowl set over a saucepan of steaming but not boiling water and melt gently (do not let the base of the bowl touch the water). Stir occasionally, until smooth. Put the eggs and maple syrup in a bowl and beat well. Add to the chocolate mixture. Stir well, and keep stirring over low heat until the mixture starts to thicken. Stir in the pecan nuts, then pour into the tart shell. Bake for 35–40 minutes until just set – the filling will still be a bit wobbly. Serve warm with the sauce and cream, if using.

When you crave the gooey texture of brownies, but in a more sophisticated package, make this divine tart with a walnut and biscuit crust.

double chocolate brownie tart with a walnut crust

150 g digestive biscuits

150 g shelled walnuts

125 g unsalted butter, melted

brownie filling

125 g dark chocolate, chopped

175 g unsalted butter, softened

400 g caster sugar

3 large eggs, beaten

1 teaspoon vanilla extract

150 g plain flour

200 g white chocolate chips

a deep cake tin, 23 cm square, base-lined with non-stick greaseproof paper

MAKES ABOUT 16 SQUARES

Crush the biscuits and walnuts in a food processor, pulsing to keep the biscuits and nuts quite coarse. Stir the biscuits into the melted butter until evenly coated. Before it cools, press evenly into the base and 4 cm up the sides of the prepared cake tin (a flat potato masher will help you to do this). Chill for 20 minutes to set the crust before filling.

Preheat the oven to 180°C (350°F) Gas 4.

To make the filling, put the chocolate in a heatproof bowl set over a small saucepan of steaming but not boiling water and melt gently (do not let the base of the bowl touch the water). Stir occasionally, until smooth. Put the butter and sugar in a bowl, cream until light and fluffy, then beat in the eggs. Stir in the melted chocolate and vanilla. Fold in the flour, then half the chocolate chips. Spoon into the tart crust and level the top. Sprinkle with the remaining chocolate chips.

Bake for 35 minutes or until a cocktail stick inserted in the middle reveals fudgy crumbs. Do not overcook.

Leave to cool in the tin, then turn out and cut into 16 pieces.

This is a cheesecake for a buffet party. It bursts with juicy pieces of tangerine, and is very refreshing after a meal. For a really special occasion, try using tangerines or clementines ready-prepared in a liqueur and sugar syrup, available from specialist grocery stores.

tangerine and chocolate cheesecake

100 g butter

225 g dark-chocolate biscuits, crushed

swirls of cream, piped chocolate decorations and tangerine segments half-dipped in chocolate, to decorate

filling

8 unwaxed tangerines (washed thoroughly if you can't find unwaxed)

25 g powdered gelatine

450 g mascarpone or full-fat soft cheese

4 eggs, separated

175 g caster sugar

300 ml crème fraîche or soured cream

3 tablespoons Cointreau or Grand Marnier

a springform cake tin, 25 cm in diameter, lined with greaseproof paper

SERVES 12

Melt the butter in a small saucepan over gentle heat, then stir in the biscuit crumbs. Press evenly into the base of the prepared cake tin and chill for 30 minutes.

To make the filling, finely grate the zest of 2 of the tangerines and set aside. Squeeze the juice from 4 of the tangerines and pour into a small saucepan. Sprinkle with the gelatine and let sponge for 10 minutes. Remove the flesh from the segments of the remaining tangerines and chop coarsely.

Put the mascarpone in a large bowl and, using a wooden spoon or electric whisk, beat until softened, then beat in the egg yolks, 100 g of the caster sugar, the crème fraîche and liqueur. Heat the gelatine slowly until dissolved, then stir into the cheese mixture. Fold in the tangerine zest and chopped tangerines.

Put the egg whites into a spotlessly clean, grease-free bowl, whisk until stiff peaks form, then gradually whisk in the remaining caster sugar. Fold into the cheese mixture and spoon into the cake tin. Level the surface and chill for 3–4 hours until set.

Carefully remove the cheesecake from the tin onto a flat serving plate. Decorate with swirls of cream topped with a chocolate decorations and chocolate-dipped tangerine segments.

A wickedly dense cheesecake to serve with the coffee after dinner. It couldn't be any easier to make. You may add any liqueur you like, but rum works particularly well. Serve in thin slices, straight from the refrigerator so that it is as cool and firm as possible.

chocolate macaroon truffle cheesecake

75 g butter

25 g soft brown sugar

175 g chocolate-coated digestive biscuits, chocolate chip cookies or chocolate bourbon biscuits, crushed

filling

250 g dark chocolate (60–70% cocoa solids), chopped

300 g full-fat soft cheese

100 g light soft brown sugar

60 ml dark rum

100 g macaroons or ratafias, finely crushed

cocoa powder, to dust

a loose-bottomed sandwich cake tin, 23 cm in diameter

SERVES 6–8

Melt the butter and sugar in a small saucepan over gentle heat. Stir in the biscuit crumbs. Press the crumb mixture thinly (you may not have to use it all) over the base of the cake tin and chill until required.

To make the filling, put the chocolate in a heatproof bowl set over a saucepan of steaming but not boiling water and melt gently (do not let the base of the bowl touch the water). Stir occasionally, until smooth.

Put the soft cheese in a large bowl and, using a wooden spoon or electric whisk, beat until softened. Beat in the brown sugar and rum, then stir in the melted chocolate and crushed macaroons. Spoon into the cake tin and level the surface as neatly as possible. Chill for 1–2 hours.

When firm, dust the top with a thin layer of cocoa powder. Carefully remove from the tin (you may like to warm the sides of the tin to release the cheesecake) and set on a large serving plate.

This creamy cheesecake holds rivulets of real raspberry and chocolate sauces in a crisp chocolatey biscuit base. Alternatively, if your time is limited, you could fold fresh raspberries and grated chocolate into the cheese mixture instead of the sauces.

raspberry and chocolate ripple cheesecake

100 g butter

2 tablespoons soft brown sugar

250 g chocolate-covered digestive biscuits, finely crushed

filling

350 g full-fat soft cheese

3 eggs, separated

100 g caster sugar

1 teaspoon vanilla extract

200 ml double cream

20 g powdered gelatine

raspberry ripple

250 g fresh or frozen raspberries

50 g caster sugar

chocolate ripple

50 g dark chocolate, chopped

2 tablespoons double cream

a loose-bottomed deep cake tin, 20 cm in diameter, greased and lined with greaseproof paper

SERVES 8

Melt the butter and sugar in a small saucepan over gentle heat. Stir in the biscuit crumbs. Press the crumb mixture evenly over the base and up the sides of the prepared cake tin. Chill for at least 30 minutes.

To make the filling, put the soft cheese in a large bowl and, using a wooden spoon or electric mixer, beat until softened. Beat in the egg yolks and half the sugar, the vanilla extract and cream.

Put the gelatine and 2 tablespoons water in a small heatproof bowl set over a saucepan of hot water and stir occasionally until the gelatine has dissolved. Keep it warm. To make the raspberry ripple, put the raspberries and sugar in a saucepan, heat gently until the sugar dissolves, then boil for 1 minute until slightly thickened. Press through a sieve and leave to cool. To make the chocolate ripple, put the chocolate and cream in another saucepan, heat until the chocolate has melted, then stir well and leave to cool until just warm, but still pourable. Beat the gelatine into the cheese mixture.

Put the egg whites in a spotlessly clean, grease-free bowl and whisk until stiff but not dry. Whisk in the remaining sugar, gradually, spoonful by spoonful, whisking until thick after each addition. Beat 2 spoonfuls of the meringue into the cheese mixture, then quickly fold in the rest. Put small spoonfuls of mixture over the biscuit case so that they join up, then pour the raspberry and chocolate sauces in between the spoonfuls of mixture. Spoon in the remaining cheese mixture and pour again (keep any remaining sauces to serve). Swirl the mixtures together with a skewer to produce a ripple effect. Give the tin a shake to settle the mixture, then chill for about 2–4 hours until set. To serve, remove the cake from the tin and carefully peel off the paper. Serve in thin slices with any extra sauces.

An outrageously rich cheesecake based on the delicious ingredients of tiramisù – coffee, mascarpone, chocolate, coffee liqueur and rum. A creamy rum and vanilla mixture is marbled through a dark chocolate, coffee and liqueur combination, then poured onto an amaretti base and baked.

tiramisù cheesecake

275 g amaretti biscuits, ratafias or macaroons, crushed

75 g unsalted butter, melted

filling

700 g mascarpone cheese or full-fat soft cheese, at room temperature

150 g caster sugar

3 eggs, separated

30 g plain flour

45 ml dark rum

½ teaspoon vanilla extract

175 g dark chocolate, chopped

1 tablespoon finely ground espresso coffee powder

3 tablespoons coffee liqueur, such as Tía María

icing sugar, to dust

a springform cake tin, 23 cm in diameter

SERVES 8–10

Stir the biscuit crumbs into the melted butter. Spoon the crumb mixture over the base of the cake tin and press evenly over the base and 4 cm up the sides with the back of a spoon to form a neat shell. Chill for at least 30 minutes until firm.

Preheat the oven to 200°C (400°F) Gas 6.

To make the filling, put the mascarpone in a bowl and, using a wooden spoon or electric mixer, beat until smooth. Add the sugar and beat until smooth, then beat in the egg yolks. Divide the mixture between 2 bowls. Stir the flour, rum and vanilla extract into one of the bowls.

Put the chocolate in a heatproof bowl set over a small saucepan of steaming but not boiling water and melt gently (do not let the base of the bowl touch the water). Stir occasionally, until smooth. Leave to cool slightly, then stir in the coffee and liqueur. Stir into the second bowl. Put the egg whites in a spotlessly clean, grease-free bowl, whisk until soft peaks form, then fold half into each cheese mixture.

Spoon alternate mounds of the cheese mixture onto the biscuit base until full. Swirl the mixtures together with a knife to produce a marbled effect (do not overmix). Bake in the preheated oven for 45 minutes until golden brown, but still soft in the centre – cover the top if it appears to be overbrowning. Turn the oven off, then leave the cheesecake in the oven with the door ajar to cool completely. Alternatively, transfer the cheesecake to a wire rack and invert a large bowl over the cake so it cools slowly. When cold, chill for several hours before serving. Serve dusted with icing sugar.

This is a very special cheesecake indeed. Make sure that the chocolate and water are melted together – the shock of adding the water later will make the chocolate thicken and seize.

chocolate marble cheesecake

100 g butter

2 tablespoons soft brown sugar

250 g chocolate-covered digestive biscuits, finely crushed

a little melted butter

100 g white chocolate, grated and chilled, to decorate

filling

150 g dark chocolate (60–70% cocoa solids), chopped

750 g full-fat soft cheese, at room temperature

250 g caster sugar

1 vanilla pod, split lengthways, seeds scraped out and set aside, or 1 teaspoon vanilla extract

2 large eggs

a springform cake tin or deep, loose-bottomed sandwich tin, 23 cm in diameter

SERVES 10

Preheat the oven to 180°C (350°F) Gas 4. Follow the instructions on page 93 to make a chocolate crumb base. Press the crumb mixture over the base of the cake tin. Bake in the preheated oven for 15 minutes, then remove from the oven, lightly firm down again and leave to cool completely. Reduce the oven temperature to 160°C (325°F) Gas 3.

When the base is cold, carefully brush the sides of the tin with a little melted butter, then chill until required.

To make the filling, put the chocolate and 50 ml water in a heatproof bowl set over a saucepan of steaming but not boiling water and melt gently (do not let the base of the bowl touch the water). Keep warm.

Put the cheese, sugar and vanilla seeds, if using, in a large bowl and, using a wooden spoon or electric mixer, beat until soft and creamy. Put the eggs and vanilla extract, if using, in a bowl and whisk well. Beat the eggs gradually into the cheese mixture. Pour 250 ml of the mixture into a jug, then pour the remaining mixture into the prepared tin.

Stir the warm dark chocolate into the reserved cheese mixture. Pour the chocolate mixture in a wide zigzag pattern over the surface of the cheesecake, edge to edge. Draw the handle of a thick wooden spoon through the pattern, zigzagging in the opposite direction so the mixtures are marbled together. Do not overwork, or the pattern will be lost. Keep it simple and the edges neat.

Bake for 20–25 minutes, or until the cheesecake starts to puff slightly around the edges but is still very soft in the centre. Transfer to a wire rack and loosen the edges with a very thin knife blade. Leave to cool slowly by putting a large upturned bowl over the cheesecake. When completely cold, chill for at least 3 hours before removing the tin. Spread the sides lightly with a very thin layer of whipped cream. Press the white chocolate around the sides. Cut with a hot knife to serve.

A semifreddo is a pudding that is half frozen to give it a slightly thickened, creamy texture. Ricotta and mascarpone are sweetened, laced with rum and Tía María, and flavoured with pulverized Italian coffee and grated dark chocolate to give an interesting texture. You must buy very finely ground espresso coffee, or it will taste gritty!

coffee ricotta semifreddo cheesecake

150 g butter

3 tablespoons soft brown sugar

375 g chocolate-covered digestive biscuits, finely crushed

125 g very cold, dark chocolate, to decorate

icing sugar, to dust

whipped cream, to serve (optional)

filling

350 g ricotta cheese, at room temperature

350 g mascarpone cheese, at room temperature

1 tablespoon dark rum

3 tablespoons coffee liqueur, such as Tía María

1 teaspoon vanilla extract

4 tablespoons icing sugar

125 g dark chocolate (60–70% cocoa solids), grated

2 tablespoons espresso ground Italian roast coffee

a springform cake tin, 25 cm in diameter, lined with greaseproof paper

SERVES 6–8

Follow the instructions on page 93 to make a chocolate crumb base. Press the crumb mixture over the base of the prepared cake tin. (Use a potato masher to flatten the crumb base evenly.) Chill until required.

To make the filling, strain the ricotta cheese into a bowl, then beat in the mascarpone cheese with a wooden spoon. (Do not attempt to do this in a food processor, otherwise the mixture will be very runny.)

Beat in the rum, liqueur, vanilla extract and sugar, then fold in the grated chocolate and ground coffee, leaving the mixture streaky. Carefully spoon onto the crumb base, leaving the surface coarse.

Freeze for about 2 hours until just frozen, not rock solid. The pudding should be only just frozen or very chilled. Transfer to the refrigerator 30 minutes before serving to soften slightly if too firm.

To serve, unmould, remove the paper and set on a large serving plate. Using a sharp knife, cut through the very cold dark chocolate to make spiky shards, then use to cover the surface of the cheesecake. Dust with icing sugar and serve with a spoonful of whipped cream, if using.

cakes & bakes

An American diner fixture, and an utterly decadent dinner finale, devil's food cake has a fine-crumbed texture and meringue-like frosting that both melt in the mouth.

devil's food counter cake with 7-minute frosting

350 ml boiling water

80 g unsweetened cocoa powder

4 eggs, at room temperature

1 tablespoon vanilla extract

350 g superfine plain flour

1 teaspoon salt

1 teaspoon bicarbonate of soda

450 g caster sugar

350 g unsalted butter, softened

7-minute frosting

300 g caster sugar

2 egg whites, at room temperature

1½ tablespoons golden syrup

¼ teaspoon cream of tartar

¼ teaspoon salt

1 teaspoon vanilla extract

3 cake tins, 20 cm in diameter, or 2 cake tins, 23 cm in diameter

SERVES 8–10

Preheat the oven to 180°C (350°F) Gas 4. Grease the cake tins and line them with greaseproof paper. Grease the paper, then dust with flour and shake off any excess.

Whisk together the boiling water and cocoa in a medium bowl until smooth. Leave to cool to room temperature. When it is cool, beat together the eggs, vanilla extract and 75 ml of the cocoa mixture.

Sift the flour, salt and bicarbonate of soda into the bowl of an electric mixer and stir in the sugar. Mix on low speed for 30 seconds, then add the softened butter and remaining cocoa liquid. Mix on low speed then turn up to medium and beat for 1½ minutes. Add the egg mixture in 3 batches, beating each one for 30 seconds. Don't overbeat. Scrape the batter into the prepared cake tins and smooth the surfaces.

Bake the cakes in the preheated oven for 25–30 minutes or until a skewer inserted into the centre of the cakes comes out clean. Rotate the cakes halfway through cooking. Leave to cool in the tins for 10 minutes then turn out onto wire racks, remove the paper and leave to cool completely. Wrap in clingfilm for up to 2 days before frosting.

To make the frosting, put 6 tablespoons water and all the ingredients except the vanilla extract in a large glass bowl set over a small saucepan of steaming but not boiling water (do not let the bottom of the bowl touch the water). Beat with an electric whisk on high speed for 7 minutes. Remove from the heat, add the vanilla extract and beat for 2 minutes more, until stiff and glossy.

Put one cake on a plate and top with frosting. Place another cake on top and spread more frosting over. Top with the last cake, if using, then frost the sides and the top. Use the back of a spoon to create peaks. The cake keeps, covered, at room temperature, for up to 2 days.

This is one of a family of meringue cakes that take their name from the flavour of buttercream used to fill them. Buttercream can be heavy and a bit fussy, so this is a less traditional version with a simple chocolate ganache, topped with whipped cream.

almond meringue and chocolate layer cake

300 ml whipping cream

2 tablespoons caster sugar

almond meringue rounds

6 large egg whites

180 g caster sugar

180 g ground almonds

2 tablespoons cornflour

chocolate ganache

400 ml double cream

300 g dark chocolate, finely chopped, plus extra to grate on top

baking trays

a piping bag fitted with a wide nozzle

SERVES 6–8

Preheat the oven to 120°C (250°F) Gas ½. Trace 3 circles, 20 cm in diameter, onto baking parchment and mark the centre point. Put the marked paper on baking trays and set aside.

To make the meringue rounds, put the egg whites and 2 tablespoons of the sugar into a spotlessly clean, grease-free bowl and, using an electric whisk, whisk until firm peaks form. Put the remaining sugar, the ground almonds and cornflour in another bowl and mix well. Gently fold the dry ingredients into the beaten whites until blended.

Transfer a third of the meringue into the piping bag. Starting in the middle of a circle marked on the baking parchment, pipe out a round, in a spiral fashion, until you reach the marked edge. Repeat to make two more rounds. Alternatively, spread the meringue inside the traced circles with a long, thin spatula, taking care to spread in an even layer so it cooks evenly. Tidy the edges. Bake in the preheated oven for 1½–2 hours until firm and dry. Leave to cool.

To make the ganache, put the cream in a saucepan and bring just to the boil. Remove from the heat and stir in the chocolate until completely melted. Leave to cool slightly.

To assemble, put one meringue layer on a serving plate. Top with a third of the ganache. Put another meringue on top, add another third of the ganache, then top with the remaining meringue and the remaining chocolate ganache. Refrigerate until the chocolate has completely cooled.

Whip the cream and sugar until firm and spread on top of the final chocolate layer. Grate some chocolate over the top and refrigerate until needed, at least 3 hours or up to 24 hours. Serve chilled.

A plain sponge cake with a big difference – cardamom. Widely used in Scandinavia and South India, this attractive pale green spice with its tiny black seeds has a unique and memorable fragrance. This simple cake is also delicious topped with icing.

chocolate, almond and cardamom cake

200 g dark chocolate, finely chopped

4 large eggs, separated

200 g caster sugar

100 g unsalted butter, very soft

100 g ground almonds

the ground black seeds from 4 cardamom pods

70 g self-raising flour

icing sugar, to dust

whipped cream or ice cream, to serve

a springform cake tin, 19 cm in diameter, greased and base-lined with greaseproof paper

MAKES ONE MEDIUM CAKE

Preheat the oven to 180°C (350°F) Gas 4.

Put the chocolate in a heatproof bowl set over a small saucepan of steaming but not boiling water and melt gently (do not let the base of the bowl touch the water). Stir occasionally, until just smooth. Remove from the heat and leave until the chocolate feels just warm. Gently stir in the egg yolks, then the sugar. Work in the butter, then the ground almonds, ground cardamom and flour.

Put the egg whites into a spotlessly clean, grease-free bowl and, using an electric whisk, whisk until stiff peaks form. Using a large metal spoon, fold the egg whites into the chocolate mixture in 3 batches.

Spoon into the prepared cake tin and bake in the preheated oven for about 1 hour or until the mixture springs back when you press it gently with your finger.

Remove from the oven, carefully turn out onto a wire rack and leave to cool. Wrap in aluminium foil, then leave overnight before cutting. Serve dusted with icing sugar and with whipped cream or ice cream. Best eaten within 5 days.

This famous pie comes from the South of the USA – it is supposed to look like the thick, dark, muddy waters of the Mississippi delta. It is very easy to make and is perfect to share with family and friends.

mississippi mud pie

base

225 g digestive or wheaten biscuits

60 g unsalted butter

60 g dark chocolate, finely chopped

filling

180 g dark chocolate, chopped

180 g unsalted butter, cubed

4 large eggs, beaten

90 g light muscovado sugar

90 g dark muscovado sugar

180 ml double cream

chocolate cream

140 ml double cream, well chilled

3 tablespoons unsweetened cocoa powder

40 g icing sugar

a springform cake tin, 23 cm in diameter, well greased

SERVES 8

Preheat the oven to 180°C (350°F) Gas 4.

To make the base, put the biscuits into a food processor and process until fine crumbs form. Alternatively, put the biscuits into a plastic bag and crush with a rolling pin. Transfer the crumbs to a mixing bowl.

Put the butter and chocolate into a heatproof bowl set over a small saucepan of steaming but not boiling water and melt gently (do not let the base of the bowl touch the water). Stir occasionally, until smooth. Remove from the heat, then stir into the biscuit crumbs. When well mixed, transfer to the prepared cake tin and, using the back of a spoon, press onto the base and about halfway up the sides of the tin. Chill while making the filling.

To make the filling, melt the chocolate and butter as above. Remove from the heat and leave to cool.

Put the eggs and sugars into a large mixing bowl and, using an electric whisk or mixer, whisk until thick and foamy. Whisk in the cream followed by the melted chocolate. Pour the mixture into the biscuit case and bake in the preheated oven for about 45 minutes until just firm. Leave to cool for a few minutes, then remove from the tin.

To make the chocolate cream, put the cream into a mixing bowl, then sift the cocoa and icing sugar on top and stir gently with a wooden spoon until blended. Cover and chill for 2 hours.

Serve the pie at room temperature with the chocolate cream. The pie can be made up to 2 days in advance and kept well covered in the refrigerator. Remove from the refrigerator 30 minutes before serving.

You can't beat a classic Black Forest Gateau, and this recipe is the one you want
for the ultimate wow-factor. The base is made the traditional way, without flour,
for a mouth-wateringly light texture.

chocolate cherry cake

9 large eggs, separated

200 g caster sugar

90 g unsweetened cocoa powder

cream and cherry filling

a 720-g jar Morello cherries in kirsch
syrup or 720-g can or jar Morello
cherries in syrup plus 3 tablespoons
kirsch (a 50-ml miniature)

425 ml double or whipping cream

3 tablespoons sugar

55 g dark chocolate, grated

*3 sandwich tins, 20.5 cm in diameter,
greased and base-lined with
greaseproof paper*

MAKES ONE LARGE CAKE

Preheat the oven to 180°C (350°F) Gas 4.

Put the egg yolks and sugar into a bowl and whisk until thick and
mousse-like – when the whisk is lifted, a wide, ribbon-like trail will
slowly fall back into the bowl. Sift the cocoa onto the mixture and
gently fold in with a large metal spoon.

Put the egg whites into a spotlessly clean, grease-free bowl and, using
an electric whisk, whisk until stiff peaks form. Carefully fold into the
yolk mixture in 3 batches. Pour the mixture into the prepared tins,
then bake in the preheated oven for 20–25 minutes until the tops of
the cakes spring back when you press them gently. Leave to cool in the
tins before unmoulding.

To make the filling, drain the cherries and save the syrup. Leave the
cherries on kitchen paper to drain. Reserve 12 to decorate.

Set one of the cooled sponges on a serving plate and sprinkle
2 tablespoons kirsch syrup over the top.

Put the cream in a bowl and, using an electric whisk or mixer, whip
until soft peaks form. Sprinkle the sugar over the cream and whip until
slightly thicker. Reserve half the cream to cover the cake. Spread half
the remaining cream over the bottom layer of sponge. Press half the
cherries into the cream.

Sprinkle the second sponge layer with 2 tablespoons kirsch syrup as
before, then gently set on top of the first layer. Spread with cream
and press in the cherries as before. Top with the last layer of sponge.
Sprinkle with 3 tablespoons kirsch syrup. Pipe or spread the top
and sides of the cake with the reserved cream, then decorate with the
reserved cherries and grated chocolate. Chill until ready to serve.
Best eaten within 48 hours.

This dark, moist chocolate cake is made all over southern Italy, but particularly in Capri. Normally it is made with ground almonds, but this recipe has been adapted to suit those who cannot eat nuts – it is equally delicious with a fantastic soft texture.

dark chocolate cake from capri

250 g unsalted butter

250 g dark chocolate (60–70% cocoa solids), chopped

4 tablespoons freshly brewed espresso

6 eggs, separated

200 g caster sugar

50 g potato flour or cornflour

½ teaspoon baking powder

150 g stale white breadcrumbs

icing sugar, to dust

whipped cream, to serve

a springform cake tin, 25 cm in diameter, sides well greased, base-lined with non-stick baking parchment

MAKES ONE LARGE CAKE

Preheat the oven to 180°C (350°F) Gas 4. Dust the prepared cake tin with flour.

Put the butter and chocolate in a heatproof bowl set over a small saucepan of steaming but not boiling water and melt gently (do not let the base of the bowl touch the water). Stir occasionally, until smooth. Remove from the heat, stir in the coffee, then leave to cool a little.

Put the egg yolks and half the sugar in a bowl and beat until pale and fluffy. Mix in the potato flour and baking powder. Carefully mix in the chocolate and butter mixture, then fold in the breadcrumbs.

Put the egg whites into a spotlessly clean, grease-free bowl and, using an electric whisk, whisk until stiff but not dry, then gradually whisk in the remaining sugar. Gently fold into the mixture. Pour into the prepared cake tin and bake in the preheated oven for about 30 minutes, until risen and almost firm in the centre. To test, insert a skewer into the middle of the cake. When removed it should have a little of the mixture clinging to it – this will ensure that the cake is moist. Do not overbake. Invert onto a wire rack to cool, then dust with icing sugar. Serve with whipped cream.

NOTE To make a smaller cake, halve the quantities and bake in a 20-cm cake tin.

Although this recipe contains cream (or half-fat crème fraîche), it doesn't require the butter used in most cakes. The highly refined white flour is also absent and instead it uses protein-packed almonds. So this is a good choice for a children's birthday cake which won't break too many nutritional rules.

chocolate and raspberry birthday cake

4 eggs

150 g golden caster sugar

100 g dark chocolate (at least 70% cocoa solids), chopped

150 g ground almonds

150 ml double cream or half-fat crème fraîche

200–300 g raspberries

two sandwich tins, 18 cm in diameter, lightly greased and base-lined with greaseproof paper

SERVES 8

Preheat the oven to 180°C (350°F) Gas 4.

Put the eggs and sugar in a heatproof bowl and place over a small saucepan of gently simmering water. Whisk with an electric whisk for 5–8 minutes until very thick and creamy. The mixture should leave a trail when it drips from the whisk. Remove the bowl from the saucepan and whisk for 3–5 minutes until cool.

Put the chocolate into a heatproof bowl set over a small saucepan of steaming but not boiling water and melt gently (do not let the base of the bowl touch the water). Stir occasionally, until smooth. Remove from the heat, then leave to cool.

Gradually add the cooled chocolate to the whisked egg mixture, stirring gently. Stir in the ground almonds, mixing lightly. Divide the mixture evenly between the sandwich tins and tap each tin lightly on the work surface to remove any air bubbles. Bake in the preheated oven for 25–30 minutes until well risen and the tops spring back when touched lightly with your finger. Remove the cakes from the oven and leave to cool in the tins for about 10 minutes before transferring them to a wire rack to cool completely. The surface will crisp up and crack as it cools. Remove and discard the greaseproof paper.

Whisk the cream, if using, with an electric whisk until soft peaks form. Spread half the cream or crème fraîche over one layer of the cake and top with half the raspberries. Put the second cake layer on top and decorate with the remaining cream or crème fraîche and raspberries. Store lightly covered in the refrigerator until required. The undecorated cake will keep for 2 days.

The most famous of all the Viennese cakes, this sumptuous chocolate cake was invented
in 1832 by the chef at the Hotel Sacher. At the hotel, you can still buy a sachertorte,
made from the original recipe and packaged in a stylish wooden box.

sachertorte

175 g dark chocolate, chopped

125 g unsalted butter,
at room temperature

150 g caster sugar

5 large eggs, separated,
plus 1 egg white

150 g plain flour

½ teaspoon baking powder

apricot glaze

4 tablespoons apricot conserve

1 teaspoon lemon juice

chocolate icing

125 ml double cream

175 g dark chocolate,
finely chopped

a little melted milk chocolate, to pipe
(optional)

whipped cream, to serve

*a springform or loose-bottomed cake
tin, 23 cm in diameter, greased and
base-lined with greaseproof paper*

*a greaseproof paper piping bag
(optional)*

SERVES 12

Preheat the oven to 170°C (325°F) Gas 3.

Put the chocolate into a heatproof bowl set over a small saucepan of
steaming but not boiling water and melt gently (do not let the base
of the bowl touch the water). Stir occasionally, until smooth. Remove
from the heat and leave to cool.

Put the butter in a large bowl and beat until creamy. Add half the sugar
and beat until fluffy. Using an electric whisk, beat in the egg yolks, one
at a time, beating well after each addition. Stir in the cooled chocolate.
Sift the flour and baking powder over and fold in with a metal spoon.

Put the 6 egg whites into a large, spotlessly clean and grease-free bowl
and, using an electric whisk, whisk until stiff peaks form, then beat in
the remaining sugar a little at a time. Fold into the chocolate mixture
in 3 batches, then spoon into the prepared tin and level the surface.
Bake in the preheated oven for 1 hour or until a skewer inserted in the
centre comes out clean. Leave to cool in the tin for 10 minutes, then
turn out onto a wire rack, remove the lining paper and leave to cool.

To make the glaze, put the conserve, lemon juice and 1 tablespoon
water into a saucepan, heat gently, then bring to the boil, stirring
constantly. Remove from the heat and strain into a bowl. Brush over
the top and sides of the cake. Leave to cool on the wire rack.

To make the icing, put the cream into a saucepan and heat until almost
boiling. Put the chocolate into a heatproof bowl and pour over the hot
cream. Leave for 2 minutes, then stir until smooth and glossy. Put a
plate under the wire rack, then pour the icing over the cake so it
covers the top and sides. Leave to set in a cool place, not the fridge.
If liked, put some melted chocolate into a piping bag and pipe the
letter 'S' on top of the cake. Serve with whipped cream. Store the cake
in an airtight container in a cool place and eat within 1 week.

Use the best-quality chocolate to produce a good flavour. The sponge can be sprinkled with rum and a little rum can also be added to the dark mousse if you like.

chocolate roulade

6 large eggs, separated

140 g icing sugar, sifted

50 g unsweetened cocoa powder

1–2 tablespoons rum (optional)

grated white chocolate and sifted cocoa powder, to decorate

dark mousse

200 g dark chocolate, chopped

100 g unsalted butter, cubed

4 large eggs, separated

1–2 tablespoons rum (optional)

1 tablespoon caster sugar

white mousse

300 ml double cream, chilled and whipped

100 g best-quality white chocolate, grated

a baking tray, 40 x 35 cm, greased and lined with greaseproof paper

MAKES ONE LARGE CAKE

Preheat the oven to 190°C (375°F) Gas 5.

Put the egg yolks and 100 g of the icing sugar in a bowl and beat until very light and mousse-like – the whisk should leave a ribbon-like trail when lifted out of the bowl. Sift the cocoa into the bowl and gently fold in with a large metal spoon. Put the egg whites in a spotlessly clean, grease-free bowl and, using an electric whisk, whisk until soft peaks form. Whisk in the remaining icing sugar, 1 tablespoon at a time, until stiff peaks form. Fold into the yolk mixture in 3 batches. Gently spread an even layer of mixture on the prepared tray, then bake in the preheated oven for 8–10 minutes until firm to the touch.

Cover a wire rack with a damp tea towel topped with a sheet of baking parchment. Tip the cooked sponge onto the rack, lift off the baking tray and peel the paper off the bottom. Leave to cool.

To make the dark mousse, put the chocolate and butter in a heatproof bowl set over a small saucepan of steaming not boiling water and melt gently. Remove from the heat and gently stir in the egg yolks, then the rum, if using. Leave to cool. Put the egg whites in a clean bowl, whisk until stiff, then add the sugar and whisk again until stiff. Fold into the chocolate mixture in 3 batches. Chill briefly until just setting.

To make the white mousse, chill the whipped cream if necessary, then fold in the grated chocolate and chill until ready to assemble.

To assemble, sprinkle the sponge with rum, if using. Spread the dark mousse mixture on top, leaving a 2-cm border of sponge all around. Cover with white mousse, then roll up from the narrow end like a Swiss roll, using the tea towel to help you. Wrap in the tea towel to give it a neat shape then chill for 30 minutes–2 hours.

When ready to serve, remove the tea towel and transfer the roll to a serving plate. Decorate with grated chocolate and cocoa powder.

This is literally a pancake-cake, layered with sweet custard and chocolate and baked in the oven.
A wedge of this curious striped chocolate pudding makes a great talking point.

chocolate galette

225 g plain flour

½ teaspoon salt

55 g caster sugar

4 eggs

550 ml milk

55 g unsalted butter,
melted and cooled

2 tablespoons brandy

peanut oil, for brushing

chocolate filling

4 egg yolks

110 g caster sugar

2 teaspoons vanilla extract

300 ml double cream

225 g dark chocolate, grated

200 g shelled walnuts,
finely chopped

*a crêpe pan or small frying pan,
20 cm in diameter*

*a springform cake tin,
20 cm in diameter, greased and
lined with greaseproof paper*

greased greaseproof paper

SERVES 8

Preheat the oven to 180°C (350°F) Gas 4.

Put the flour into a food processor, add the salt, sugar, eggs, milk, cooled melted butter and brandy and pulse for a few seconds until smooth. Heat the crêpe pan, brush with peanut oil, then wipe away any excess with kitchen paper. Spoon 2 tablespoons of the batter into the hot pan and quickly swirl it around to coat the base of the pan evenly but thinly. If you add too much batter, just tip the extra back into the bowl and trim away the pouring trail. Cook the crêpe for 1 minute, then carefully turn it over and cook the other side. You should have at least 15, depending on how thin you make them.

To make the filling, put the egg yolks and sugar into a bowl and whisk until pale and thick. Beat in the vanilla extract and cream.

Put a crêpe in the base of the prepared cake tin, spread it with a little vanilla cream mixture and sprinkle with grated chocolate and walnuts. Repeat the layers until you run out of crêpes or fill the tin. Finish with a crêpe and cover it with a piece of greased greaseproof paper.

Bake in the preheated oven for 30 minutes. Remove from the oven and leave to cool slightly before unclipping the tin and transferring the galette to a serving plate.

Linzertorte is a classic dish dating back to the glory days of the Austrian Empire, and traditionally made from a nutty shortbread-like pastry and raspberry conserve. This recipe is not authentic, but fresh raspberries are the perfect contrast to the ultra-rich pastry.

raspberry and chocolate linzertorte

230 g shelled hazelnuts

110 g unsalted butter, at room temperature

100 g icing sugar, sifted, plus extra to sprinkle

3 large egg yolks

200 g plain flour

½ teaspoon baking powder

2 teaspoons ground cinnamon

¼ teaspoon grated nutmeg

25 g unsweetened cocoa powder

vanilla ice cream or whipped cream, to serve

raspberry filling

1½ tablespoons cornflour

3 tablespoons caster sugar, or to taste

600 g raspberries

a loose-bottomed flan tin, 23 cm in diameter, well greased

SERVES 8

Preheat the oven to 180°C (350°F) Gas 4.

Put the hazelnuts in an ovenproof dish and toast in the preheated oven for about 15 minutes or until light golden brown. If they still have their papery brown skin, put them in a clean, dry tea towel, then gather up the ends and rub the hazelnuts together to loosen the skins. Leave to cool, then transfer the hazelnuts to a food processor and grind to a fine powder. Keep the oven on.

Put the butter into a mixing bowl and beat until creamy. Add the icing sugar and beat, slowly at first, until fluffy. Beat in the egg yolks one at a time, beating well after each addition. Sift the flour, baking powder, cinnamon, nutmeg and cocoa onto the mixture and work in using a wooden spoon. Finally, add the ground nuts and work in, using your hands to bring the pastry together.

Take three-quarters of the pastry and crumble it into the prepared tin. Using your fingers, press the pastry over the base and up the sides to cover the inside of the tin completely and form a layer about 1 cm thick. Chill for 15 minutes. Put the remaining pastry onto a well floured work surface and roll out, slightly thinner, to a rectangle about 23 x 14 cm. Cut into strips about 1 cm wide.

Sprinkle the cornflour and sugar over the raspberries and toss gently until almost mixed. Transfer the filling into the pastry case and spread it gently and evenly.

Arrange the lattice strips over the filling – if the pastry breaks, just push it back together again. Bake in the preheated oven for about 25–30 minutes, until the pastry is a slightly darker brown and just firm. Leave to cool, then remove from the pan and serve sprinkled with icing sugar. Best eaten the same day. Not suitable for freezing.

Just what you need with ice cream and bananas. If you can take the egg whites out of the fridge for an hour before you start it helps a lot. A rotary whisk or electric mixer or whisk and spotlessly clean, grease-free, bowl are essential to beat the whites to a stiff snow.

chocolate meringues

75 g good dark chocolate, chopped

3 egg whites

a pinch of cream of tartar

175 g caster sugar

non-stick greaseproof paper

2 baking trays

MAKES 12

Preheat the oven to 120°C (250°F) Gas ½.

Cut out 2 rectangles of non-stick greaseproof paper to fit your baking trays, then put one on each tray.

Put the chocolate in a heatproof bowl set over a small saucepan of steaming not boiling water and melt gently (do not let the base of the bowl touch the water). Stir occasionally, until smooth. Remove from the heat and leave to cool slightly while you whisk up the whites.

Put the egg whites and cream of tartar into a large, spotlessly clean, grease-free bowl and, using an electric whisk, whisk until stiff. Tip the sugar onto the whites and whisk until stiff and glossy.

Drizzle the melted chocolate over the meringue then gently stir through, using very few strokes so the mixture looks very streaky and marbled.

Scoop a heaped tablespoon of the mixture out of the bowl and drop onto one of the prepared baking trays. Repeat with the rest of the mixture to make 12, spacing them slightly apart on the trays.

Put the meringues in the preheated oven for 2 hours. Remove the trays from the oven and leave to cool. Peel the meringues off the lining paper and serve. Store in an airtight container for up to 1 week.

These pastry puffs filled with chocolate are a little like the delicious French pastry, *pain au chocolat*. Making them with frozen puff pastry is even faster than a trip to the *pâtisserie*. If you prefer, you can use dark chocolate instead of the white.

spiced white chocolate puffs

2 sheets ready-rolled puff pastry, thawed if frozen

plain flour, to dust

175 g white chocolate, cut into 24 squares

ground mixed spice, to dust

1 egg yolk

2 tablespoons milk

cocoa powder, to dust

MAKES 8

Preheat the oven to 220°C (425°F) Gas 7. Grease a baking tray.

Put the pastry on a floured work surface and cut each sheet into 4 pieces, 10 cm square.

Put 3 pieces of chocolate onto each square, then add a light dusting of mixed spice (use a small tea strainer). Dampen the edges with a little water, then fold them over diagonally to form a triangle. Press the edges together to seal, then, using the blade of a sharp knife, gently tap the sealed edges several times (this will help the pastry rise).

Transfer the triangles to the prepared baking tray. Put the egg yolk and milk into a small bowl, beat well, then brush over the pastry. Bake in the preheated oven for 10–15 minutes until risen and golden.

Remove from the oven, leave to cool for 5 minutes, lightly dust with cocoa powder and serve with coffee.

Some brownie enthusiasts believe that only cocoa should be used, not melted dark chocolate, as it gives a deeper, truly intense chocolate flavour which balances the sugar necessary to give a proper fudgy texture. Choose the best-quality cocoa you can find.

old-fashioned brownies

100 g walnut pieces

4 large eggs

300 g caster sugar

140 g unsalted butter, melted

½ teaspoon vanilla extract

140 g plain flour

75 g unsweetened cocoa powder

a brownie tin, 20.5 x 25.5 cm, greased and base-lined with greaseproof paper

MAKES 16

Preheat the oven to 170°C (325°F) Gas 3.

Put the walnut pieces in an ovenproof dish and lightly toast in the preheated oven for about 10 minutes. Remove from the oven and leave to cool. Keep the oven on.

Meanwhile, break the eggs into a mixing bowl. Use an electric whisk to whisk until frothy, then whisk in the sugar. Whisk for a minute then, still whisking constantly, add the melted butter in a steady stream. Whisk for a minute, then whisk in the vanilla extract.

Sieve the flour and cocoa into the bowl and stir in with a wooden spoon. When thoroughly combined stir in the nuts. Transfer the mixture to the prepared tin and spread evenly. Bake in the preheated oven for about 25 minutes until a skewer inserted halfway between the sides and the centre comes out just clean. Remove from the oven.

Leave to cool completely before removing from the tin and cutting into 16 pieces. Store in an airtight container and eat within 5 days.

This recipe is for those seasoned brownie fans who want to try something a bit different. It's really like a fun version of after-dinner mints. You'll need a box (or bar) of bitter-sweet dark chocolate with a soft, mint-flavoured fondant centre, of the type that is most often sold as 'after-dinner' mints.

mint brownies

125 g dark chocolate (60–70% cocoa solids), chopped

100 g unsalted butter, cubed

3 large eggs

200 g caster sugar

100 g plain flour

2 tablespoons unsweetened cocoa powder

100 g–200 g bitter-sweet dark chocolate with mint centre (depending on strength of flavour required)

a brownie tin, 20.5 x 25.5 cm, greased

MAKES 20

Preheat the oven to 180°C (350°F) Gas 4.

Put the chocolate and butter in a heatproof bowl set over a small saucepan of steaming not boiling water and melt gently (do not let the base of the bowl touch the water). Stir occasionally, until smooth. Remove from the heat and leave to cool.

Whisk the eggs, then add the sugar and whisk until thick and mousse-like. Whisk in the melted chocolate mixture. Sift the flour and cocoa onto the mixture and stir in. When thoroughly combined spoon half the brownie mixture into the prepared tin and spread evenly.

Leave the mint chocolates whole or break them up (depending on the size of the ones you are using). Arrange them over the brownie mixture already in the tin. Spoon the remaining brownie mixture on top and gently spread to cover the chocolate mints.

Bake in the preheated oven for about 25 minutes or until a skewer inserted halfway between the sides and the centre comes out just clean (though some of the sticky mint layer will appear). Remove the tin from the oven.

Leave to cool before removing from the tin and cutting into 20 pieces. Store in an airtight container and eat within 5 days.

Here an easy all-in-one brownie mixture is made thinner and more pliable than usual,
then sliced up and sandwiched with vanilla ice cream. Note that it must be frozen for at least
6 hours before serving.

brownie ice-cream cake

200 g dark chocolate (60–70%
cocoa solids), chopped

75 g unsalted butter, cubed

150 g caster sugar

2 large eggs, lightly beaten

½ teaspoon vanilla extract

100 g plain flour

½ teaspoon baking powder

75 g toasted almonds,
finely chopped

1 litre good-quality vanilla ice cream

Creamy Chocolate Sauce
(page 151), to serve

*a Swiss roll tin, 30.5 x 20.5 cm,
greased and base-lined with
greaseproof paper*

SERVES 8

Preheat the oven to 170°C (325°F) Gas 3.

Put the chocolate, butter and 2 tablespoons water in a heatproof bowl
set over a small saucepan of steaming not boiling water and melt gently
(do not let the base of the bowl touch the water). Stir frequently, until
smooth. Add the sugar and stir well to thoroughly combine. Remove
the bowl from the pan and leave to cool for a couple of minutes.

Stir in the eggs and vanilla extract and mix well. Sift the flour and
baking powder onto the mixture and mix in. Finally, stir in the nuts.
Transfer the mixture to the prepared tin and spread evenly.

Bake in the preheated oven for about 15–20 minutes or until a skewer
inserted into the centre of the mixture comes out just clean. Leave to
cool completely in the tin, then turn out onto a chopping board.

Cut the brownie in half lengthways to make 2 long strips. Cut one of
the strips into 8 equal pieces. Wrap the long strip and the 8 top pieces
in foil and freeze until firm. When ready to assemble, transfer the ice
cream to the fridge to slightly soften (it must not be allowed to melt).
Put the long brownie strip onto a freezerproof serving platter or baking
tray, then pile the ice cream on top and quickly neaten the sides and
top. Arrange the 8 brownie pieces on top. Return to the freezer until
firm then wrap tightly and freeze for at least 6 hours before serving.

When ready to serve, use a sharp knife to cut into 8 portions and offer
a jug of Creamy Chocolate Sauce for pouring. The assembled cake can
be kept in the freezer for up to 1 week.

This attractive blondie – a brownie made with white chocolate instead of dark – is studded with fresh raspberries and makes a heavenly summer dessert. It is rich but not too heavy. Serve with a fresh raspberry sauce (for example the Melba Sauce on page 155) and vanilla ice cream.

white chocolate and raspberry blondies

250 g good-quality white chocolate

200 g unsalted butter, cubed

3 large eggs

150 g caster sugar

½ teaspoon vanilla extract

200 g plain flour

1 teaspoon baking powder

150 g raspberries

a brownie tin, 20.5 x 20.5 cm, greased and base-lined with greaseproof paper

MAKES 9

Preheat the oven to 180°C (350°F) Gas 4.

Break up 150 g of the chocolate and put it in a heatproof bowl with the butter. Set over a small saucepan of steaming but not boiling water and melt gently (do not let the base of the bowl touch the water). Stir frequently, until smooth. Remove the bowl from the pan and leave to cool until needed.

Break the eggs into the bowl of an electric mixer or a mixing bowl. Whisk until frothy then add the sugar and vanilla extract and beat thoroughly until very thick and mousse-like.

Whisk in the melted chocolate mixture. Sift the flour and baking powder onto the mixture and fold in. Chop the rest of the chocolate into pieces the size of your little fingernail and stir them in. Spoon the mixture into the prepared tin and spread evenly. Scatter the raspberries over the top.

Bake in the preheated oven for about 25 minutes or until a skewer inserted halfway between the sides and the centre comes out just clean. Leave to cool before removing from the tin and cutting into 9 large pieces. Store in an airtight container and eat within 2 days.

An irresistible combination of filo pastry, nuts and rich dark chocolate makes this pudding a firm favourite at every dinner party. Serve with plenty of whipped cream. For best results, use only good-quality chocolate and very fresh nuts and, before using the filo pastry, make sure it has properly thawed, according to the instructions on the packet.

nut and chocolate strudel

100 g blanched almonds

100 g shelled unsalted pistachios

100 g walnut pieces

75 g unsalted butter

75 g light muscovado sugar

75 g dark chocolate

200 g filo pastry, thawed if frozen

whipped cream, to serve

cinnamon syrup

110 g caster sugar

1 cinnamon stick

1 teaspoon freshly squeezed lemon juice

2 tablespoons clear honey
or maple syrup

a large roasting tin, well greased

SERVES 6–8

Preheat the oven to 180°C (350°F) Gas 4.

Put all the nuts into a food processor and chop until they resemble coarse breadcrumbs. Put the nuts into a heavy-based, dry frying pan and stir over low heat until just starting to colour. Because nuts scorch quickly, it's best to undercook slightly, rather than risk overcooking them. Remove from the heat and stir in the butter and sugar. Leave to cool. Using a sharp knife, chop the chocolate the same size as the chopped nuts, then mix with the nuts.

Unwrap the filo pastry and put onto a clean work surface. Overlap the sheets to make a large rectangle about 90 x 65 cm.

Sprinkle the filling evenly over the pastry, then carefully roll up. Arrange in a horseshoe shape in the prepared roasting tin, tucking the ends under neatly. Bake in the preheated oven for about 25 minutes or until the top is crisp and light golden brown. Remove from the oven and leave to cool in the tin while making the syrup.

To make the syrup, put the sugar and 100 ml water into a medium, heavy-based saucepan and heat gently, stirring frequently, until dissolved. Bring to the boil, then add the cinnamon stick, lemon juice and honey and simmer for 10 minutes until syrupy. Leave to cool for 5 minutes, then remove the cinnamon stick and pour the hot syrup over the strudel. Leave to cool so the strudel can absorb the syrup, then cut into thick slices and serve with piles of whipped cream. Best eaten within 24 hours. Not suitable for freezing.

This deliciously rich and indulgent chocolate log is hard to resist and creates a tempting sweet treat at Christmas time. For a tasty variation, use tinned sweetened chestnut purée for the filling, in place of the whipped cream. Children especially will love this cake and it provides an ideal alternative for those who are not so keen on Christmas cake.

bûche de noël

3 eggs

115 g caster sugar, plus extra to sprinkle

85 g plain flour

2 tablespoons unsweetened cocoa powder

1 tablespoon hot water

300 ml double cream

chocolate icing

55 g dark chocolate, chopped

115 g unsalted butter, softened

225 g icing sugar, sifted, plus extra to dust

1 tablespoon milk

a Swiss roll tin, 33 x 23 cm, greased and lined with non-stick baking parchment

SERVES 8–10

Preheat the oven to 200°C (400°F) Gas 6.

Put the eggs and sugar in a large bowl. Whisk together using an electric whisk at high speed until the mixture is pale, fluffy and thick enough to leave a trail on the surface when the whisk is lifted. Sift half the flour and cocoa powder over the mixture and fold it in very gently but thoroughly using a large metal spoon. Sift in the remaining flour and cocoa powder and fold in until evenly mixed. Fold in the water.

Pour the mixture into the prepared tin, tilting it backwards and forwards to spread the mixture evenly. Bake in the preheated oven for 10–12 minutes or until the sponge springs back when lightly pressed.

Turn the cake out onto a sheet of greaseproof paper sprinkled with caster sugar and set on a damp tea towel. Trim the crusty edges, then roll up the cake from a short side with the paper inside and leave to cool on a wire rack.

To make the icing, put the chocolate in a heatproof bowl set over a small saucepan of steaming but not boiling water and melt gently (do not let the base of the bowl touch the water). Stir frequently, until smooth. Beat the butter until pale and fluffy, then gradually stir in the icing sugar. Add the melted chocolate and milk and beat until light and smooth. Whip the cream in another bowl to form stiff peaks.

Unroll the cake, remove the paper and spread with the whipped cream. Roll it up neatly from a short side and place it on a cake board. Cut a thick diagonal slice off one end and attach it to one side with a little chocolate icing, to resemble a branch. Spread the remaining icing evenly over the whole cake, then score the surface with a fork to resemble bark. Chill in the refrigerator, if liked.

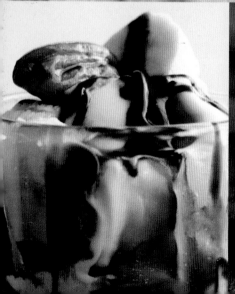

on the side

Real vanilla is expensive, but the process that takes it from plant to table is so complex, there is little wonder. Don't be tempted to save money by using cheap, inferior imitation vanilla, the results simply won't be the same. However, do rinse and dry the pods, then bury them deep in a jar of sugar to flavour it in readiness for your next batch of ice cream. There is simply nothing which better complements a chocolate dessert than good vanilla ice cream.

rich vanilla ice cream

2 vanilla pods
300 ml whole milk
300 ml double cream
6 large egg yolks
150 g caster sugar

an ice-cream machine (optional)

SERVES 4–6

Split the vanilla pods lengthways and scrape out the seeds with the tip of a knife. Put the pods in a saucepan and the seeds in a bowl.

Pour the milk and cream into the saucepan with the vanilla pods and bring just to boiling point. Remove from the heat and set aside to infuse for at least 30 minutes.

Put the eggs and sugar in a bowl and beat until pale and creamy. Return the cream mixture to the heat and bring back to the boil. Pour the hot liquid over the eggs, stir until smooth, then pour back into the pan. Reduce the heat and cook over low heat, stirring constantly with a wooden spoon, until the custard has thickened enough to leave a finger trail on the back of the spoon. Take care that the mixture doesn't overheat and scramble.

Leave the custard to cool completely, then churn in an ice-cream machine and transfer to a freezerproof container and freeze until ready to serve. Alternatively, to freeze without a machine, put the custard in a shallow, freezerproof container and freeze until almost solid. Remove from the freezer, beat well with a wire whisk or electric whisk until smooth, then return to the freezer. Repeat the process twice more to break down the ice crystals, and the result will be silky ice cream.

NOTE If you have time, the custard will benefit by being left for several hours before churning, to let the flavours develop fully.

This is the ultimate indulgence! Serve drizzled over vanilla ice cream or chocolate brownies.

maple and pecan fudge sauce

75 g unsalted butter

75 ml maple syrup

75 ml double cream

75 g shelled pecan nuts

SERVES 6–8

Heat the butter, maple syrup and cream together over low heat until the butter has melted. Increase the heat and simmer fast for 5 minutes, or until the sauce is thick. Stir in the pecans and simmer for a further minute. Leave to cool for 15–20 minutes and serve warm.

NOTE If you make this sauce in advance and leave it to cool completely, warm it through before serving.

Crème anglaise or custard should be stirred constantly over very gentle heat otherwise the egg yolks can curdle and spoil the sauce. It is such a versatile sauce that it goes well with a variety of hot and cold chocolate puddings.

crème anglaise

600 ml milk

1 vanilla pod, split lengthways

6 egg yolks

2 tablespoons caster sugar

SERVES 8–10

Put the milk and vanilla pod in a saucepan and set over very gentle heat until it reaches boiling point. Remove from the heat and set aside to infuse for 20 minutes, then discard the vanilla pod.

Whisk the egg yolks and sugar together in a bowl until pale and creamy, then stir in the infused milk. Return to the pan and cook, stirring constantly with a wooden spoon. Do not let the sauce boil.

When the mixture has thickened so that it coats the back of the spoon, remove from the heat. If you plan to serve it cold, cover the surface with clingfilm to prevent a skin from forming while it cools.

Whisked egg whites are the basis for these crisp tuile biscuits. The mixture must be spread thinly, baked until light brown, then quickly draped over an orange to give a basket shape. The biscuits can also be rolled up. Don't worry if the first couple you make are not perfect – you'll soon get the hang of it. Serve them filled with a scoop of ice cream and drizzled with chocolatey sauce.

chocolate baskets

2 large egg whites

110 g caster sugar

55 g plain flour

55 g unsalted butter, melted and cooled

30 g dark chocolate, very finely chopped

grated zest of 1 unwaxed orange

several baking trays, lined with non-stick greaseproof paper

MAKES ABOUT 16

Preheat the oven to 180°C (350°F) Gas 4.

Put the egg whites into a spotlessly clean, grease-free bowl and, using an electric whisk, whisk until stiff peaks form. Whisk in the sugar. Sift the flour onto the whites, gently fold it in using a large metal spoon, then fold in the cooled, melted butter, chocolate and orange zest.

Put a scant tablespoon of the mixture onto a prepared baking tray and spread thinly with the back of a spoon to make a 12-cm disc. Make another disc in the same way, then bake in the preheated oven for 7–10 minutes until lightly browned. Continue making and baking 2 discs at a time.

Using a palette knife, carefully lift each tuile off the baking tray and, while still hot, drape over an orange so it cools and sets in a basket shape. The hot tuiles can also be rolled around the handle of a wooden spoon to make thin, crisp, rolled-up biscuits. If the tuiles become too cool to shape, return them to the oven for 1 minute to soften. Store in an airtight container. Best eaten within 24 hours.

The classic sauce for steamed puddings, such as the wonderful Chocolate, Orange and Date Steamed Pudding on page 20.

chocolate custard sauce

450 ml milk

3 tablespoons unsweetened cocoa powder

60 g caster sugar

1 tablespoon cornflour

2 egg yolks

SERVES 4–6

Put all but 2 tablespoons of the milk into a large, heavy-based saucepan and heat until almost boiling. Sift the cocoa, sugar and cornflour into a heatproof bowl, stir in the egg yolks and the 2 tablespoons cold milk to form a thick paste, then stir in the hot milk. Strain the mixture back into the saucepan and stir constantly over low heat until the mixture thickens – do not let the mixture boil or it will curdle.

Remove from the heat and use immediately, or keep it warm until ready to serve.

Both these cones and wafers are the perfect way to provide an extra dose of chocolate for the truly committed chocolate lover. Simple and endlessly satisfying.

chocolate ice-cream cones

100 g dark chocolate, chopped

8 ice-cream cones

a pastry brush

several baking trays, lined with non-stick greaseproof paper

MAKES 8

Put the chocolate in a heatproof bowl set over a small saucepan of steaming but not boiling water and melt gently (do not let the base of the bowl touch the water). Stir occasionally, until smooth.

Using a pastry brush, brush the inside of the cones with the melted chocolate. Arrange on the baking trays and leave to set in a cool place (or the refrigerator in very hot weather).

chocolate ice-cream wafers

175 g plain flour

a pinch of salt

½ teaspoon baking powder

25 g unsweetened cocoa powder

110 g caster sugar

125 g unsalted butter, cubed

1 teaspoon vanilla extract

several baking trays, lined with non-stick greaseproof paper

MAKES 14–16

Preheat the oven to 200°C (400°F) Gas 6.

Sift the flour, salt, baking powder, cocoa and sugar into a food processor. Add the butter and vanilla extract and process until the dough comes together into a ball. Shape into a brick, about 10 x 7 x 5 cm. Wrap in greaseproof paper and chill until firm. Using a sharp knife, cut the dough into wafer-thin slices. Set apart on the baking trays and bake in a preheated oven for about 5–7 minutes until just firm and the edges are starting to colour. Leave to cool for 2 minutes until firm enough to transfer to a wire rack.

Best eaten within 5 days. The dough can be kept in the refrigerator for up to 1 week or frozen for up to 1 month.

A lovely thick and rich hot sauce that's not too sweet.

chocolate fudge sauce

175 g dark chocolate (60–70% cocoa solids), chopped

40 g unsalted butter, cubed

2 tablespoons golden syrup

175 ml single cream or milk

SERVES 4–6

Put the chocolate, butter, golden syrup and cream in a small, heavy-based pan. Set over low heat and melt gently, stirring constantly. Continue stirring and heating until the mixture is almost at boiling point. Pour into a warm jug and serve immediately.

The sauce thickens as it cools but can be gently reheated. Any leftover sauce can be covered and stored in the fridge for up to 2 days. Reheat gently before using.

A deliciously rich sauce and more classic version of the Maple and Pecan Fudge Sauce on page 145.

butterscotch fudge sauce

90 g unsalted butter, cubed

200 g dark or light brown muscovado sugar

2 tablespoons golden syrup

90 ml double cream

SERVES 6

Put the butter, sugar and golden syrup in a small, heavy-based pan. Melt gently over very low heat, stirring frequently, until the sugar dissolves completely (about 10 minutes). When smooth and melted, stir in the cream then raise the heat and stir until the sauce is piping hot but not boiling. Pour into a warm jug and serve immediately.

Any leftover sauce can be covered and stored in the fridge for up to 3 days. Reheat gently before using.

A simple yet rich sauce without added sugar – the ideal counterbalance to a particularly sweet dessert or a dollop of the Rich Vanilla Ice Cream on page 143.

creamy chocolate sauce

125 ml double cream

85 g dark chocolate (60–70% cocoa solids), finely chopped

½ teaspoon vanilla extract

SERVES 4–6

Pour the cream into a small, heavy-based saucepan and heat gently, stirring frequently. When it comes to the boil, remove the pan from the heat and leave to cool for a minute. Stir in the chocolate and vanilla extract and keep stirring until smooth. Pour into a warm jug and serve immediately. The sauce thickens as it cools but can be gently reheated.

Any leftover sauce can be covered and stored in the fridge for up to 2 days. Reheat very gently, stirring constantly, before using.

Choose top-quality white chocolate flavoured with real vanilla pods (rather than children's bars) for a good rich taste.

white chocolate sauce

200 g good-quality white chocolate, chopped

200 ml double cream

80 ml milk

1 vanilla pod, split lengthways

SERVES 4–6

Put the chocolate in a heatproof bowl set over a small saucepan of steaming but not boiling water and melt gently (do not let the base of the bowl touch the water). Stir frequently, until smooth. Remove the bowl from the pan and leave to cool until needed.

Put the cream, milk and vanilla pod into a small, heavy-based pan. Heat, stirring constantly, until scalding hot but not quite boiling.

Remove from the heat and leave to stand for 5 minutes. Remove the vanilla pod then pour the hot cream and milk onto the melted chocolate in a thin stream, whisking constantly, to make a smooth sauce. Pour into a warm jug and serve immediately.

Any leftover sauce can be stored, tightly covered, in the fridge for up to 2 days. Reheat very gently, stirring constantly.

Use good, well-flavoured coffee but not espresso (or dilute espresso until it tastes like filter or cafetière coffee).

coffee sauce

100 g dark chocolate (60–70% cocoa solids), chopped

60 g unsalted butter, cubed

100 ml freshly brewed, good coffee

SERVES 4–6

Put the chocolate, butter and coffee in a heatproof bowl set over a small saucepan of steaming but not boiling water and melt gently (do not let the base of the bowl touch the water). Stir frequently, until smooth. Remove the bowl from the pan. As the sauce cools it will become even thicker. Serve warm.

Any leftover sauce can be stored, tightly covered, in the fridge for up to 2 days. Reheat very gently, stirring constantly.

This tangy passion fruit syrup is sublime poured over vanilla ice cream or fresh fruit pavlova. The sweetest, ripest passion fruit have a very dimpled skin – be sure to buy them like this.

passion fruit sauce

100 g caster sugar

75 ml passion fruit pulp
(from about 6 passion fruit)

SERVES 4

Put the sugar and 100 ml water in a saucepan and heat gently until the sugar dissolves. Add the passion fruit pulp, bring to the boil, then simmer gently for 10 minutes, or until the fruit mixture is reduced slightly and has thickened. Leave to cool and serve at room temperature.

In this tempting sauce, fresh blueberries are simmered until they burst and release their juices and luscious flavours. Serve with cream-based puddings such as panna cotta or lemon posset.

blueberry sauce

350 g fresh blueberries

3 tablespoons caster sugar

grated zest of ½ unwaxed lemon

a squeeze of fresh lemon juice

SERVES 4

Put the blueberries, sugar, lemon zest and 1 tablespoon water in a saucepan and heat gently until the sugar dissolves. Increase the heat slightly and simmer, partially covered, for 8–10 minutes, or until the berries soften and the sauce thickens.

Remove from the heat and add the lemon juice. Serve hot or leave to cool and serve at room temperature.

This fresh raspberry sauce was traditionally served with peaches and cream to make peach Melba, but it is equally delicious with any other fresh fruit, such as strawberries or blueberries. Alternatively, serve it with ice cream or the White Chocolate and Raspberry Blondies on page 135.

melba sauce

250 g raspberries

2 tablespoons kirsch

1–2 tablespoons icing sugar

SERVES 4–6

Put all the ingredients in a food processor and blend until smooth. Pass the purée through a fine sieve and serve.

Pastry can be made by hand, or in a food processor. If you have cool hands, the hand method
is best because more air will be incorporated. If you have hot hands, the food processor is
a blessing. The quantities of water added vary according to the humidity of the flour,
so always add less than the recipe says – you can add more if the dough is dry.

sweet rich shortcrust pastry

250 g plain flour

2 tablespoons icing sugar

½ teaspoon salt

125 g unsalted butter,
chilled and cubed

2 egg yolks

2 tablespoons iced water

**MAKES ABOUT 400 G PASTRY,
ENOUGH TO LINE A TART TIN
23–25 CM IN DIAMETER OR
TO MAKE A DOUBLE CRUST
FOR A DEEP PIE PLATE
20–23 CM IN DIAMETER**

Sift the flour, icing sugar and salt together into a bowl, then rub in
the butter. Mix the egg yolks with the 2 tablespoons iced water. Add
to the flour, mixing together lightly with a knife. The dough must
have some water in it or it will be too difficult to handle. If it is still
too dry, add a little more water, sprinkling it over the flour mixture
1 tablespoon at a time.

Transfer the mixture to a lightly floured work surface. Knead lightly
with your hands until smooth. Form the dough into a rough ball.
Flatten slightly, then wrap in clingfilm and chill for at least 30 minutes
before rolling out.

This is the classic French sweet pastry sometimes known as *pâte sablée* or 'sandy pastry', because it has a fine crumbly texture when broken. Its high sugar content means that it can burn very easily – use a timer. It takes slightly longer to blind bake than other pastries – bake at the standard 190°C (375°F) Gas 5 for 15 minutes, then reduce the temperature to 180°C (350°F) Gas 4 and cook for a further 10 minutes to dry out completely.

pâte sucrée

200 g plain flour

a pinch of salt

75 g caster or icing sugar

75 g unsalted butter, cubed,
at room temperature

2 egg yolks

½ teaspoon vanilla extract

2–3 tablespoons iced water

MAKES ABOUT 400 G PASTRY,
ENOUGH TO LINE A TART TIN
25 CM IN DIAMETER OR
6 TARTLET TINS 9 CM IN
DIAMETER

CLASSIC METHOD Sift the flour, salt and sugar into a mound on a clean work surface. Make a well in the middle with your fist.

Put the butter, egg yolks and vanilla extract in the well. Using the fingers of one hand, 'peck' the eggs and butter together until the mixture resembles creamy scrambled eggs.

Flick the flour over the egg mixture and chop it through with a palette knife or pastry scraper, until it is almost amalgamated but looking very lumpy. Sprinkle with the water and chop again.

Bring together quickly with your hands. Knead lightly into a ball, then flatten slightly. Wrap in clingfilm, then chill for at least 30 minutes before using. Leave to return to room temperature before rolling out.

FOOD PROCESSOR METHOD Put the sugar, butter, egg yolks and vanilla extract in a food processor, then blend until smooth. Add the water and blend again.

Sift the flour and salt onto a sheet of greaseproof paper, then add to the processor. Blend until just combined. Transfer the dough to a lightly floured work surface. Knead gently until smooth. Form into a flattened ball, then wrap in clingfilm. Chill or freeze for at least 30 minutes. Leave to return to room temperature before rolling out. This is quite a delicate pastry to roll, so be sure to use enough (but not too much) flour when rolling.

Index

Recipe Credits

SUSANNAH BLAKE
Dark chocolate, prune and armagnac mousses
Chocolate, coffee and vanilla bombe
White chocolate and Kahlúa mousse torte

TAMSIN BURNETT-HALL
White chocolate and raspberry fools

MAXINE CLARK
Pear and chocolate crumble
Dark chocolate risotto
Pain au chocolat pudding
Chocolate, orange and date steamed pudding
Dracula's delight
Banana and chocolate tarte Tatin
Tiramisù with raspberries
Profiteroles con sorpresa
Baked darkest chocolate mousse tart
Lemon and almond tart with a chocolate amaretti crust
Strawberry chocolate tartlets
Chocolate pecan tart with coffee bean sauce
Double chocolate brownie tart with a walnut crust
Pâte sucrée
Sweet rich shortcrust pastry
Tangerine and chocolate cheesecake

Chocolate macaroon truffle cheesecake
Raspberry and chocolate ripple cheesecake
Tiramisù cheesecake
Chocolate marble cheesecake
Coffee ricotta semifreddo cheesecake
Dark chocolate cake from Capri

LINDA COLLISTER
Brownie lava pudding
Old-fashioned brownies
Mint brownies
Brownie ice-cream cake
White chocolate and raspberry blondies
Chocolate fudge sauce
Butterscotch fudge sauce
Creamy chocolate sauce
White chocolate sauce
Coffee sauce
Chocolate fondue
Chocolate soufflés
Very rich chocolate brûlées
White and black puddings
Pistachio and chocolate ice cream
Italian chocolate and hazelnut torta
Mississippi mud pie
Sachertorte
Raspberry and chocolate linzertorte
Nut and chocolate strudel

Chocolate baskets
Chocolate custard sauce
Chocolate ice-cream wafers
Chocolate ice-cream cones
Chocolate, almond and cardamom cake
Chocolate cherry cake
Chocolate roulade
Chocolate meringues

CLARE FERGUSON
Bitter chocolate and hazelnut gelato

LIZ FRANKLIN
Rich vanilla ice cream

KATE HABERSHON
Chocolate galette

RACHAEL ANNE HILL
Hot Jamaican chocolate bananas
Chocolate and raspberry birthday cake

JENNIFER JOYCE
Nutella and bananas on brioche
Banana splits with hot fudge sauce
Devil's food counter cake with 7-minute frosting

JANE NORAIKA
Strawberries and cherries in tricolour chocolate

ELSA PETERSEN-SCHEPELERN
Rocky road ice cream
Mint chocolate chip ice cream
Chocolate chip cookie ice-cream sandwiches

LOUISE PICKFORD
Spiced white chocolate puffs
Crème anglaise
Maple and pecan fudge sauce
Blueberry sauce
Melba sauce
Passion fruit sauce

ANNE SHEASBY
Bûche de Noël

SARA JAYNE STANES
Little hot chocolate mousses
White chocolate mousses
Chocolate marquise

FRAN WARDE
Upside-down fruit pudding

LAURA WASHBURN
Chocolate cream pots
Chocolate chestnut tart
Almond meringue and chocolate layer cake

Photography Credits

CAROLINE ARBER
Page 8ac, 19

MARTIN BRIGDALE
Pages 8ar, bc & br, 13, 24, 27, 31, 34al, cl, c, & bc, 37, 38, 41, 44, 48, 54, 58, 63, 65, 68a & b all, cl &cr, 70, 73, 75, 76, 81, 82, 85, 87, 88, 91, 92, 95, 97, 98, 101ac, cl & cr, 102, 105, 109, 117, 123, 137, 138, 140ac, c, cr & bc, 146, 147, 148, 149, 156, 157

PETER CASSIDY
Endpapers, pages 1, 4-5a, 5, 8al & c, 10, 14, 21, 34bl, 50, 68c, 78, 127

JEAN CAZALS
Page 101ar, 112

NICKI DOWEY
Page 22

RICHARD JUNG
Pages 2, 3, 6, 7, 8cl & cr, 16, 29, 34ar, 53, 57, 101bc & br, 128, 131, 133, 134, 140al & ar, 151, 153

WILLIAM LINGWOOD
Pages 42, 120, 140cl, 142

NOEL MURPHY
Page 114

WILLIAM REAVELL
Pages 8bl, 32, 34ac, 47

DEBI TRELOAR
Pages 34cr & br, 60, 66, 101ar, c& br, 106, 111, 119

IAN WALLACE
Pages 140bl & br, 144, 154

POLLY WREFORD
Page 124